E

Featuring the foods, beverages, dining specialties and customs of 19 Spanish speaking countries including:

Argentina	*Mexico*
Bolivia	*Nicaragua*
Chile	*Panama*
Columbia	*Paraguay*
Costa Rica	*Peru*
Dominican Republic	*Puerto Rico*
Ecuador	*Spain*
El Salvador	*Uruguay*
Guatemala	*Venezuela*
Honduras	•

Soon to be available in the

The *What Kind of Food Am I?* Series

•

THE WHAT KIND OF FOOD AM I? SERIES

EATING & DRINKING IN SPANISH

*Reading Menus in
Spanish Speaking Countries*

Andy Herbach and Michael Dillon

CAPRA PRESS
SANTA BARBARA

For our families and friends

Special thanks to Jeanne Cohen

•

Cover design and illustrations
by Michael Dillon.

LIBRARY OF CONGRESS
CATALOGING-IN-PUBLICATION DATA

Herbach, Andy.
    Eating & drinking in Spanish : reading menus in
Spanish speaking countries / Andy Herbach, Michael Dillon.
        p. cm. -- (The What kind of food am I? series)
    ISBN 0-88496-411-6 (pbk.)
    1. Food--Dictionaries--Spanish. 2. Cookery--
Dictionaries--Spanish. 3. Spanish language--Dictionaries--
English. I. Dillon, Michael. II. Title. III. Series.
TX350.H39 1996
641.5946'03--dc20   96-28234
                                                         CIP

CAPRA  PRESS

Post Office Box 2068
Santa Barbara, CA 93120

Contents

The *What Kind of Food Am I?* Series

Eating and Drinking in Spanish

Introduction

If you love to travel as we do, you know the importance of a good guide. The same is true of dining. A good guide can make all the difference between a memorable evening and a dizzyingly bad one. This simple translation dictionary is a means to finding your way around a menu that is entirely in Spanish. Instead of fumbling with a bulky, conspicuous tourist guide (most of which usually include a very incomplete listing of foods) in a restaurant, this book is a pocket sized alphabetical listing of food and drink commonly found on menus in Spanish speaking countries.

Of course, traveling to a foreign country means something different to everyone. For every vacation there are different expectations, different needs, and every traveler has his or her own idea of what will make that vacation memorable. For us, the making of a memorable vacation begins and ends with food.

Oh sure, the Louvre is great but have you ever had one of those long skinny hot dogs they sell in the little stands around Paris? They're bubbling hot, buried under a layer of delicately golden brown swiss cheese. We can't remember if we saw the Mona Lisa at the Louvre but we know for sure that we had one of those delicious hot dogs (not a thing like American hot dogs, not that we have anything against them) right after we came out of a grueling afternoon looking at art. We sprinted through the Prado (considerably faster than we are capable of running any 10K) and then sat down to a memorable pizza at a stunning little restaurant about a block away. The owner was exceptionally charming. We ate there twice while in Madrid, the second time greeted like old friends. We spent exactly one day in Turkey and have a vague memory of the little coastal town we visited but we clearly remember the boiling hot cauldron of peculiar organ meat stew the waiter proudly presented to us. We could only choke down a few bites. We'd rather have this authentic memory of Turkey than an American style lunch any day. This, to us, is travel.

If your idea of a vacation is an all-inclusive resort, you may not need this book. (Not that we have any objection to vacations of this nature, we don't, and in fact, we would happily leave on one right this instant, if the opportunity presented itself). We are not the most adventurous people in the world, but we do enjoy getting a taste of the culture of the country we are visiting. We'd sooner visit a great little restaurant than a museum any day. You can always see that Goya in a book but reading about wood roasted wild boar just doesn't deliver.

Unfortunately, even people who speak passable Spanish can have trouble reading a menu. Although you may know that the word for meat in Spanish is *carne*, you might be surprised to discover *vieja ropa* (which means "old clothes") on a menu. In fact, it is shredded beef. This guide was created for the not-altogether adventurous traveler who wants to know what he or she is eating, but is afraid to, or cannot ask. We know the panic of opening a menu without recognizing one word on it and the disappointment of being served something other than what you thought you'd ordered. On our first trip to Europe, we were served a plate of cold brains, we thought we had ordered chicken.

The next time you find yourself seated in a red tiled courtyard with bougainvillea cascading over whitewashed walls and the scent of *comidas hispanicas* in the night air and an incomprehensible menu in your hands, simply pull this guide from your pocket and get ready to enjoy the delicious cuisine of the country you are exploring.

pollo

Spanish food is not the same as Mexican food although that is a common misconception. Although Spanish food may sometimes be spicy, it is not hot.

A meal in Spain consists of two courses, dessert and coffee. The first course is often soup, stew or *paella*. The second course is either fish or meat.

Paella was invented in Valencia on the southeastern coast. There are said to be over 1500 variations of *paella*, a popular national dish of saffron flavored rice and various ingredients. Saffron is the costliest spice in the world since it must be harvested by hand. Spain produces more saffron than any other country.

Spanish cuisine varies by region. In southern Andalucia, you will find seafood and *gazpacho*. There are many variations of this cold soup. The most common is tomato-based. Three ingredients are found in all variations: bread, vinegar and oil. The word *gazpacho* derives from *caspa*, which means leftovers or crumbs. The food in Catalonia, bordering on France, is similar to the cuisine of French Provence. Don't miss the fish stews such as *zarzuela*.

In northern Asturias, you will find hearty stews such as *fabada*, a stew made with ham, sausage and white beans. Shellfish dominates the cuisine of Northwest Spain (Galicia). The cuisine of Navarra and Aragon (in the North of Spain bordering France) stresses vegetables, chicken and pepper sauces. The Basques like roasted foods and sauces, along with some of the finest seafood dishes.

Lamb, pork and game dishes are popular in Extremadura in Western Spain, along with *jamón serrano* (the popular cured ham of Spain). Roasted meats (*asados*) are the specialty in the center of Spain (Castilla or Castile).

The Spaniards love *tapas*. They are small amounts of nearly any kind of food usually served with a small glass of wine. The time between lunch and dinner is usually when most Spaniards frequent *tapas* bars. You can have a *porción* (small sample) or a *ración* (a larger quantity). *Tapas* bars are open all day. The word *tapa* means lid or cover and comes from the practice of covering the jugs of wine w/pieces of food on toast or plates.

If you are concerned about the cost of a meal, the *menú del dia* (menu of the day) is usually a better value for your money than purchasing food á la carte.

Like most restaurants in Europe, Spanish restaurants almost always post their menus outside, usually near the front door or in a window.

Tipping

Restaurants automatically include a tax and service charge. It is still customary to leave a small tip unless the service or the food has been unsatisfactory.

It is always safe to ask if the tip is included. (*¿Esta incluida la propina?*)

Mealtimes

It cannot be stressed enough that Spaniards eat extremely late. The midday meal is usually served between 1:00 p.m. and 4:00 p.m. The evening meal is served between 10:00 p.m. and midnight. While some restaurants in the larger cities have begun to open earlier, especially in restaurants that are frequented by tourists, most Spaniards like to eat late and you'll find a more genuine Spanish dining experience if you do too.

Drink

Spanish wines are gaining popularity. The town of Valdepeñas produces the most table wines. Rioja is the most popular of the more expensive wines. *Reserva* or *Gran Reserva* on a wine bottle means that the wine is a better wine. The Spaniards love sherry (or *jerez*,

10

as it is called in Spain) and there are several good national and local beers (*cervezas*). Throughout Spain, you will find many varieties of *sangria*, a wine and fruit punch. The menu reader portion of this guide also includes beverages, both alcoholic and non-alcoholic.

Water

Europeans joke that you can tell a U.S. tourist from his fanny pack, clothes and ubiquitous bottle of mineral water. Tap water is safe in all parts of Spain, but mineral water is often served with meals.

SOUTH AMERICA

Since the food and drink in the Spanish speaking countries of South America are extremely varied, we've included a brief and not-at-all comprehensive description of each country's cuisine.

Venezuela
Columbia
Ecuador
Peru
Bolivia
Paraguay
Chile
Uruguay
Argentina

Argentina

Argentine cuisine can be characterized as meat, meat and more meat! The national dishes of Argentina are usually a composite of Spanish and Italian food. Try the *parillada* (mixed grill), *ñoquis* (Italian gnocchi or potato dumplings) and the *pucheros* (hearty stews). Although Chilean wines may be better known, Argentina produces world-class wines. Only France, Italy, Spain and the United States produce more wine annually and only the French and Italians drink more wine per capita.

Bolivia

Lunch is usually the main meal of the day in Bolivia. Hot red peppers are found in many Bolivian dishes. Seafood is not as common

11

in Bolivia as it is a landlocked nation. Try the ever-present *chuños* (freeze dried potatoes), *empanada salteña* (a spicy turnover filled with ground meat, peppers, chicken, diced potatoes, onions, olives and raisins), *fricassé* (pork cooked in a spicy sauce and served with potatoes and corn) and *sopa de maní* (roasted peanut soup).

Chile

The cuisine of Chile is quite international and its wines are respected the world over. Because of Chile's long coastline, seafood is abundant. *Albacora* (swordfish), *corvina* (sea bass) and *chupe de mariscos* (seafood stew) are only a few of the seafood dishes you will find here. The beef in Chile is generally not considered to be of the same quality as in Argentina and Uruguay. Tea time, called "*once*" is popular. *Once* refers to snacks served in the late afternoon or early evening. At this time, tea or coffee is served with cookies, toast, cheese or other small appetizers similar to the British "elevenses" or tea time. *Once* means eleven and *aguardiente* (the national "fire water") has eleven letters. So, when someone says that he is having his "*once*", it may also mean that he is having a drink of *aguardiente*.

Columbia

Columbians eat large and spicy evening meals. Breakfast and lunch are generally light meals. *Arroz con pollo* (rice and chicken) is found on almost every menu. Try *puchero bogotano* (boiled vegetables, meat and potatoes), *piquete* (meat, vegetables and potatoes in a spicy, hot pepper sauce) and *bandeja paisa*, (also called *plato montañero*), (a dish with ground beef, sausage, salt pork, beans, rice, avocado and fried egg).

Ecuador

The food in Ecuador is not spicy. Shrimp and lobster are abundant as are many delicious tropical fruits. Try *llapingachos*

12

(mashed potatoes w/cheese), *locro* (a corn or potato soup w/cheese and avocados) and *yaguarlocro*, potato soup w/black pudding (blood sausage).

Paraguay

Note: Unlike most other South American countries, the service charge is frequently not added to the bill. Paraguayan restaurants feature beef, pasta and *empanadas* (turnovers). Try the national dishes of *sooyosopy* (soup containing cornmeal, ground meat and usually served with rice) and *sopa paraguaya* "paraguayan soup" (mashed cornbread, cheese, onion, milk and eggs). The national "fire water" is *caña*, an alcoholic beverage made from sugar cane and similar to rum.

Peru

In coastal areas, seafood dominates. Since pepper and garlic are popular, Peruvian cuisine is extremely hot. Vegetables and tropical fruits are abundant. Try *ají de gallina* (chicken in a hot pepper and cheese sauce), *lomo saltado* (stir-fried steak served w/onions, rice, tomatoes and vegetables) and *pisco* (the national "fire water"). Because of the large Asian population in Peru, you will find many Chinese restaurants or *chifas*.

Uruguay

Lunch is often a large and long meal in Uruguay. Beef dominates the cuisine. Dinner is almost always served extremely late. Don't miss *carbonada* (meat and rice stew with pears, peaches and raisins), *chivito al plato* (steak topped with a fried egg and served with potato salad, a green salad and french fries), *milanesa* (breaded and fried veal cutlet), *morcilla dulce* (sweet blood sausage) and *olímpicos* (club sandwiches).

Venezuela

Venezuelan cuisine is quite continental. You will find steaks, seafood, many Italian restaurants and a Caribbean influence in the cuisine of Venezuela. Try *parrilla criolla* (marinated beef cooked on a grill), *pasticho* (a dish which is very similar to lasagna), *sancocho* (a vegetable based stew which contains any combination of chicken, meat and/or fish) and *muchacho* (beef loin roasted and served in a sauce). Pass on the *lapa*, it's a large fried rodent.

Tipping

In South America, tips and service charges are often included in restaurant and bar bills with Paraguay being the exception. Always check your bill to determine if service (*servicio*) is included. It is customary to tip 10%. Of course, if the service is especially good, you may give more.

Mealtimes

Lunch is generally a much larger meal in South America. Breakfast tends to be light, especially in Argentina, since dinner is eaten quite late (rarely before 9:00 p.m). Lunch is almost always the main meal of the day in Chile and in Ecuador.

Water

Most cities in South America have adequate tap water. Such is not the case in areas outside of major cities. Don't drink the water anywhere in Ecuador. To order juice and to make sure tap water has not been added to concentrate, ask for *jugo puro sin agua* ("pure juice without water"). Salmonella is also a concern in outlying areas, so make sure your meats and eggs are thoroughly cooked ("*bien cocido*" or well done). We prefer to play it safe and drink only mineral water. Although the list is long, remember many food and drinks may have been made or washed with contaminated water, like fruit juices made from concentrate. Salads and fruits should be washed with purified water. Peeled fruits are the safest. Remember to consider if the ice in your cocktail was made from tap water. Make sure that the water used for tea and coffee

14

has been adequately boiled. It is not unknown for unscrupulous restaurant owners to fill mineral water bottles with plain tap water. The best precaution is to make sure the bottle is sealed when it is brought to your table.

CENTRAL AMERICA

Eggs and beans (*huevos y frijoles*) are the staples of Central American cuisine. *Tortillas* (corn meal pancakes) are almost always included in any meal along with *salsa picante* (hot sauce). *Comedores* (local restaurants) allow you to sample *huevos y frijoles*, usually along with cheese and meat. Remember that in Central America, if you plan on dining at a restaurant that caters to tourists, you are almost always going spend much more money than you would at *comedores*. *Comida típica* is a basic menu found in *comedores* and consists of meat, beans and rice.

Guatemala
El Salvador
Honduras
Nicaragua
Costa Rica
Panama

Costa Rica

Although it is served all day long, *gallo pinto* (mixed cooked beans and rice) is the national breakfast of Costa Rica and is served everywhere. *Bocas* are appetizers served w/alcoholic beverages. *Casados* (fish, meat or chicken with rice, beans and a cooked vegetable, usually served with a small salad) is a common inexpensive evening meal. It means "married people". Other specialties include: *guiso de maíz* (thick corn stew), *horchata* (clear, sometimes dangerous alcoholic beverage, made from corn), *tamales* (chicken or pork w/rice, olives and raisins stuffed in cornmeal and wrapped in banana leaves (the *tamal*)) and *olla de carne* (beef stew usually with plantains and yucca).

El Salvador

Seafood (lobster, shrimp, crab, corvina and robalo) dominates the cuisine of El Salvador. Strangely, despite this country's past rela-

15

tions with the United States, fast food restaurants from the United States are everywhere and quite popular. Some specialties include *pupusas* (fried *tortillas* filled with cheese, beans and/or meat) and you will find them everywhere, *minutas* (honey flavored drink made with crushed ice), watch out for the purity of the water, and *horchata* (rice based sweet beverage usually served in a plastic bag. Again, watch out for the purity of the water).

Guatemala

Comedores are found everywhere and usually serve only *comida típica*. *Boquitas* are small appetizers such as olives, peanuts or crackers. *Tuntas* (freeze dried potatoes) are served w/many dishes. Other specialties include *antojito* (*tortilla* sandwich filled with beef, tomatoes and onions), *carne guisada* (sauce with stewed beef), *chirmol* (grilled steak served with tomato and onion sauce), *chuchitos* (meat & sauce stuffed in dough & wrapped in a corn husk), *fiambre* (meat, fish and cheese salad), *mosh* (oats with honey and cinnamon). For the true travel experience, I suppose some might want to try *tepezcuintle* (a Mayan specialty consisting of the largest member of the rodent family).

Honduras

Comedores serve *plato típico* (a combination of rice, meat, beans, cheese, tortillas and eggs). On the coast, inexpensive seafood is prevalent. Some specialties are: *anafre* (bean paste smothered with melted cheese), *pinchos* (a dish similar to shish kebabs) and *sopa de mondongo* (tripe stew or soup). *Pupusas* (like those found in El Salvador, but almost always filled with pork) are found everywhere.

Nicaragua

Plato típico is a large inexpensive meal containing any of the following: beans, rice, meat, fried plantains, *tortillas*, cheese and a salad. It is served at most inexpensive restaurants. *Gallo pinto* (beans and rice) is found everywhere as are *nacatamales* (*tortillas* filled w/meat-usually pork-corn and a sauce and steamed in banana leaves or a corn husk). Seafood is abundant near the coast and is usually served in a garlic sauce (*al ajillo*). Some other specialties are: *pana de coco* (coconut bread), *tajaditas*, (fried plantain chips) and *tortillas con quesillo* (fried corn *tortillas* with melted cheese between).

Panama

Panama means "abundance of fish", so don't miss *ceviche* (marinated raw fish appetizer) and *corvina* (sea bass). Specialties include *ropa vieja* (rice topped with spicy shredded beef and green peppers. The term means "old clothes"), *sancocho* (a spicy stew of meat and vegetables) and *arroz con coco y titi* (rice w/coconut and shrimp). For dessert try *arroz con cacao* (chocolate flavored rice pudding). *Langosta* (lobster) and *gambas* (shrimp) are served everywhere.

Tipping

Tipping can be extremely confusing in Central America. As a general rule, tipping is not expected in cheaper restaurants, but is greatly appreciated. In more expensive restaurants, a tip is expected and often included in your bill. It is typical for a *impuesto de valor agregado* (IVA) to be added to your restaurant bill. The typical IVA is from 7 - 10%. Ten to fifteen percent is a reasonable tip in most Central American countries, except in Panama, where the expected tip is 15%. Your restaurant bill in Costa Rica will already have added a 10% tip (in addition to a tax). You may want to add an additional 5%. In Guatemala, tipping is optional and not expected unless you are dining in a higher priced restaurant. A 10% tip may have already been added to your bill. In Honduras and Nicaragua, tipping is also not expected except for in higher priced restaurants where it is often included in the bill. In El Salvador, food is extremely inexpensive. Accordingly, at least a 10% tip is common. In more expensive restaurants, it probably will be added to your bill. Have we

17

thoroughly confused you now? We always leave at least a 10% tip no matter where we eat and usually it is more like 20% given the low price of meals in many parts of South and Central America.

Mealtimes
Similar to the United States and Canada.

Water
We would never drink any water unless we are absolutely sure that it is safe. The general rule is to only drink mineral water.

All water must be purified in Guatemala, Honduras and (depending who you talk to) in El Salvador. Although water is said to be safe in the major cities of other Central American countries, why risk it?

Additional precautions are listed in the "water" section of the South American portion of this guide.

Puerto Rico

Puerto Rico

The cuisine of Puerto Rico has been influenced by Spain, the Caribbean and Africa. This combination of influences makes Puerto Rican cuisine varied and unique. Of course, due to its commonwealth status, the cuisine has also been influenced by the United States. Some of the finest fresh seafood dishes are found along Puerto Rico's 270 mile coast. *Criolla* cuisine blends the influences of Spain, Africa and Taino and Arawak Indian foods. Some specialties include: *asopao* (a thick stew made of rice and w/chicken, pork or fish. Puerto Rico's most popular native dish), *encebollado* (steak smothered in onions), *surrullitos* (deep fried corn sticks stuffed with cheese) and *serenata* (cod in a vinaigrette sauce with onions, avocados and vegetables). Don't miss *tembleque* (coconut pudding) and *cocos fríos* (cold drinking coconuts).

As in the United States, a 15% to 20% tip is expected. Service is
rarely included.

Mealtimes
Similar to mealtimes in the United States and Canada.

Water
Most people drink the tap water in Puerto Rico without problems.
However, if you have a sensitive stomach, it is recommended that
you drink bottled water.   *Hispaniola*

Dominican Republic

The cuisine of the
Dominican Republic also
combines Spanish,
Caribbean and African cuisine. In resorts,
travelers will find international cuisine. Outside of resorts, international cuisine is not common. The Dominican Republic, despite an
increasing United States influence, has several noteworthy local
dishes. *Arroz con habichuelas* (rice and beans are served with
nearly everything), *asopao* (a thick stew made with rice and with
meat or seafood, similar to the Puerto Rican national dish of the
same name), *calabaza* (a squash served with many dishes), *cocos
frios* (cold green drinking coconuts), *sopa criolla dominicana* (a
soup of stewed meat, greens, onions, spices and pasta. The meat
can be anything), *langosta* (some of the finest lobster is here) and
plátanos (plantains). Often, they are baked and called *plátanos
horneados)*. Don't miss *quesillo de leche y piña,* (caramel custard
of milk and pineapple)

Tipping
The tax referenced on your restaurant bill includes a 10% service
charge and a tax. You may also want to leave an additional 5-10%
for good service

Although tourist restaurants may open for dinner at 6:00 p.m., locals do not eat until much later, 9:00 or 10:00 p.m.

Water

Do not drink the tap water in the Dominican Republic. Be careful with salads and fruits and read the sections of this guide discussing water in South and Central America and Mexico.

Mexico

Corn is the staple of Mexican cooking. *Tortillas*, *tacos* and *enchiladas* dominate the Mexican table. Visitors from the United States are generally familiar with Mexican food. Of course, some have the misconception that Mexican food is the same as tex-mex, which it is not. All Mexican food is not hot and Mexican cooks do not use chili in everything. Mexican food is a combination of Indian dishes and Spanish cuisine. Some Mexican specialties are *chimichangas* (deep fried *tortilla* stuffed with beef, beans, chilies and spices), *huachinango* (red snapper), *gorditas* (small, thick *tortillas* fried w/chopped meat, cheese, vegetables, shredded lettuce and chili sauce on top), *guacamole* (dip of mashed avocado, tomato, onion, cilantro & chilies), *huevos rancheros* (fried eggs served w/a hot tomato sauce), *pollo borracho* (fried chicken in a tequila based sauce, means "drunken chicken") and *cocada* (coconut cooked w/sugar, egg yolks and sherry).

Tipping

In a restaurant, you should tip 15% - 20%. Remember, waiters and waitresses depend on tips, as most restaurants do not pay, or pay an extremely small, hourly wage.

Mealtimes

Lunch is usually the largest meal of the day and is eaten between 2:00 p.m. and 4:00 p.m. Dinner is not served until 9:00 p.m. or 10:00 p.m., with the exception of restaurants in tourist areas.

Water

What more can be said than "Turista, play it safe." Don't drink the water (and remember this includes ice), don't brush your teeth with tap water, be careful with salads and fruits and read the sections of this guide discussing water in South and Central America. Don't ruin your vacation by failing to follow these simple precautions.

Buen Provecho
(Bon Appetit)

Speaking Spanish - Pronunciation Guide

If you are looking for a comprehensive guide to speaking Spanish, this is not the the right place. What follows is simply a few tips for speaking Spanish and a very brief pronunciation guide.

It is always good to learn a few polite terms so that you can excuse yourself when you've stepped on the foot of an elderly lady or spilled your drink down the back of the gentleman in front of you. It's also just common courtesy to greet the people you meet in your hotel, in shops and restaurants in their own language.

The Spanish language is actually very straight forward. Unlike English, every letter is pronounced in Spanish, even the final vowels on words ending with *e*'s. The one major exception is the double L which is pronounced like a *y* (tortilla) in Central and most of South America, or *sh,* in Spain and some parts of South America.

The last syllable is stressed in words ending with a consonant except *n* and *s*.

The next to the last syllable is stressed in words ending with *n* and *s* and in words ending in a vowel.

If a word is an exception to the above rules, an accent appears over the vowel of the stressed syllable.

a like *ah*.

b usually as in English, but sometimes like a *v*.

c similar to the English *k*.

– Before *e* and *i*, similar to the English *s* or *th* (in Spain).

ch the same as in English.

d similar to the English d, except at the end of a word or between vowels, like th.

e like e in they.

f the same as in English.

g like g in gate.

– Before *e* and *i*, like the English j.

h not pronounced in Spanish.

i like the English ee.

j like a throaty h.

k the same as in English (and in words of foreign origin).

l the same as in English.

ll like a *y* in Central and most of South America, like an *sh* in Spain and some of South America.

m the same as English.

n the same as English.

ñ like a combination of *n* and *y* as in canyon.

o like *oh*.

p the same as English.

q pronounced like a k.

r pronounced like an *r* with the tip of the tongue against the ridge of the gums.

rr a strong rolled r sound.

s the same as English.

t the same as English.

u like the u in crude.

v like the English *b*, except like the English *v* within a word.

w the same as in English (and only found in words of foreign origin).

y the same as in English, except when alone like ee in meet. In Argentina and Uruguay like a combination of *j* and *z*.

z like *th* in Spain and like *s* in all other spanish speaking countries.

English to Spanish

This is a brief listing of some familiar English food and food related words that you may need in a restaurant setting. It is followed by a list of phrases that may come in handy.

anchovies, anchoas

appetizer, una tapa

    (Latin America), saladito

apple, manzana

artichoke, alcachofa

ashtray, cenicero

asparagus, espárragos

avocado, aguacate.

    (Latin America), palta

bacon, tocino/beicon

baked, al horno

banana, banana. Do not confuse
    this w/*plátano*

beans, frijoles/habichuelas

beef, carne de vaca/buey

beefsteak, bistec/biftec

beer, cerveza.

    (Chile), chop or schop.

    (Venezuela), lisa

beverages, bebidas

bill, la cuenta

bitter, amargo

boiled, hervido

bottle (half), media botella

bottle, botella

bowl, tazón

bread rolls, panecillos/pancitos

bread, pan

breakfast, desayuno

broiled, asado

broth, caldo

butter, mantequilla.

    (Latin America), manteca

cabbage, repollo/col

cake, una torta/un pastel

candle, vela

carrot, zanahoria

cereal, cereal

chair, silla

check, la cuenta

cheers, salud

cheese, queso

cherry, cereza

chicken soup, caldo de
    gallina/sopa de pollo

chicken, pollo

chops, chuletas

clams, almejas

cocktail, aperitivo/cóctel

cod, bacalao

coffee, café

coffee w/hot water (to dilute),
    café con agua caliente

coffee w/milk, café con leche

coffee (black), café negro

coffee (decaf), café descafeinado

coffee (small cup) w/milk or
    cream, café cortado

cold, frío

condiments, condimentos

corn, maíz

cottage cheese, requesón

cover charge, cubierto

cucumber, pepino

cup, taza

custard, natillas

demitasse/black coffee, café solo

dessert, postre

dinner, cena/comida

dish (plate), plato

drinks, bebidas

duck, pato

eggs, huevos

espresso, café exprés

fish, pescado

fish soup, sopa de pescado

fork, tenedor

fowl, gallina

french fries, patatas fritas.
    (Latin America), papas fritas

fresh, fresco

fried, frito

fruit, frutas

game, carne de caza

garlic, ajo

gin, ginebra

glass, vaso

glass w/stem, copa

goat (baby), cabrito

grapefruit, pomelo/toronja

grapes, uvas

green beans, judías verdes

grilled, a la parilla/plancha

ham (boiled), lacón

ham (cured), jamón

hamburger, hamburguesa

honey, miel

hors d'oeuvres, entremeses

hot, caliente

ice, hielo

ice coffee, café granizado

ice cream, helado

ice (on the rocks), con hielo

ice water, agua helada

iced tea, té helado

ketchup, salsa de tomate

knife, cuchillo

lamb, cordero

large, grande

lemon, limón

lettuce, lechuga

little (a little), poco

liver, hígado

lobster, langosta

loin, lomo

lunch, almuerzo

24

mango, mango
marinated, escabeche
matches, fósforo/cerilla
mayonnaise (with), alli olli
meat, carne
medium (cooked), regular/un
poquito crudo
melon, melón
menu, la carta/el menú
milk, leche
mineral water, agua mineral
mineral water (sparkling), agua
mineral gaseoso or con gas
mineral water (w/out carbona-
tion), agua mineral sin gas
mixed, mixta
mushrooms, setas/champiñones
mussels, mejillones
mustard, mostaza
napkin, servilleta
noodles, tallarines
octopus, pulpo
oil, aceite
olive oil, aceite de oliva
omelette, tortilla.
(Latin America), tortilla de huevos
on the rocks (w/ ice), con hielo
onions, cebollas
orange, naranja
orange juice, jugo de naranja
overdone, demasiado hecha

oysters, ostras
partridge, perdiz
pastries, pasteles
peaches, melocatones
pears, peras
peas, guisantes
pepper (spice), pimienta
peppers (vegetable), pimientos
perch, mero
pineapple, piña
plantains, plátanos
plate (dish), plato
please, por favor
plums, ciruelas
poached, hervido
pork, cerdo/puerco
potatoes, patatas.
(Latin America), papas
poultry, aves
prawns, langostinos
quail, codorniz
rabbit, conejo
rare, cruda/poco hecha
raspberry, frambuesa
receipt, recibo
rice, arroz
rice pudding, arroz con leche
roasted, asado
salad, ensalada
salt, sal
salty, salado

sandwich, sandwich, bocadillo or torta

sauce, salsa

saucer, platillo

sautéed, salteado

scallops, vieiras

scrambled, revuelto

seafood, mariscos

seasonings, condimentos

sherry, jerez

shrimp, camarones/gambas

small, pequeño

smoked, ahumado

snails, caracoles

sole, lenguado

soup, sopa/caldo

sparkling (wine), espumoso

specialty, especialidad

spinach, espinaca

spoon, cuchara

squid, calamares

steak, filete

steamed, cocido al vapor

stewed, estofado

strawberries, fresas

sugar, azúcar

sugar substitute, sacarina

supper, cena

sweet, dulce

table, mesa

tea, té

tea w/lemon, té con limón

tea w/milk, té con leche

teaspoon, la cucharilla

tenderloin, solomillo/filete

thank you, gracias

tip, propina

toasted, tostado

tomato, tomate

trout, trucha

tumbler (glass), vaso

tuna, atún/bonito

turkey, pavo

utensil, utensilio

veal, ternera

vegetables, legumbres/verduras

vegetarian, vegeteriano

venison, venado

vinegar, vinagre

vodka, vodka

waiter, camarero/señor.

 (Arg., Urug. & Chile), el garzón.

 (C. America & Mexico), el mesero.

 (Latin America), el mozo.

 (Venezuela), el mesonero

waitress, camarera/señora or señorita.

 (C. America & Mexico), la mesera.

 (Arg., Urug. & Chile), la garzona.

 (Latin America), la moza

water, agua

watermelon, sandía

well done, muy hecho/bien cocido

whipped creme, nata

wine, vino

wine (full-bodied), vino de cuerpo

wine list, carta de vinos

wine (red), vino tinto

wine (rosé), clarete.

    (Latin America), rosé

wine (white), vino blanco

yogurt, yogar

---

please, por favor

thank you, gracias

a table, please, una mesa,
    por favor

I want to reserve a table, quiero
    reservar una mesa

for one person, para una persona

for two persons, para dos personas
    tres (3), cuatro (4), cinco (5),
    seis (6), siete (7), ocho (8),
    nueve (9), diez (10)

this evening, esta noche

tomorrow, mañana

the day after tomorrow, pasado
    mañana

near the window, cerca de
    la ventana

outside, a fuera

inside, dentro

on the patio, en el patio

on the balcony, en el balcón

w/a view, con una vista

no smoking, no fumar (don't
    count on this in any
    Spanish speaking country)

where is?, ¿donde esta?

the bathroom, el cuarto de baño
    (los servicios)

The bill please, la cuenta, por favor

a mistake (error), un error

Is service included?, ¿Está el
    servicio incluido? or ¿Está
    incluida la propina?

Do you accept credit cards?,
    ¿Aceptan tarjetas de crédito?

Do you accept traveller's checks?,
    ¿Aceptan cheques de viaje?

What is this?, ¿Qué es esto?

I did not order this, No pedí esto

This is, Esto está

too, demasiado

cold, fría/frío

spicy, picante

not fresh, no está fresco

not cooked, no está hecho

burnt, quemado

very good, muy bueno

delicious, delicioso or rico

a caballo, steak topped w/eggs

a punto, medium done

a su gusto, your own way

abadejo, fresh cod

aberezada, with dressing

aberezo de la mesa, condiments

abichón, sand smelt

abocado, semi-sweet table wine

acedera, sorrel

acedia, baby sole

aceite, oil

aceite de girosol, sunflower oil

aceite de oliva, olive oil

aceite de palma, palm oil

aceite de soja, soy bean oil

aceituna, olive.

aceituna negra, black olive

aceituna verde, green olive

aceitunas aliñadas, olives w/salad dressing

aceitunas rellenas, stuffed olives

acelga, beet greens/beets/Swiss chard

acerola, *(Puerto Rico)* wild cherry

achicoria, chicory/endive

achiote, *(Mexico, Puerto Rico)* annatto seed paste

aderezo (de mesa), condiments

adobo, marinated prior to cooking. *(Puerto Rico)* garlic & oregano marinade.

   (Mexico) chili & vinegar marinade

adobos de carne, meat marinades

agridulce, sweet and sour

A caballo means ∴ on horseBack

Aciete, the word for oil, is derived from Acietuna, the word for olive.

Spain is the world's largest producer of olives.

28

agua, water

agua de azahar, orange or
    lemon blossom water

agua de coca, *(Central America)* coconut water

agua de panela, *(Latin America)* drink made
    from water & sugar

agua de sel, seltzer or soda water

agua destilada, distilled water

agua dulce, *(Costa Rica)* boiled water w/brown sugar

agua fresca, *(Mexico)* sweet, water-based
    beverage flavored w/fruit

agua helada, ice water

agua mineral, mineral water

agua mineral con gas, mineral water (sparkling)

agua mineral gaseoso, mineral water (sparkling)

agua mineral sin gas, mineral water (w/out carbonation)

agua potable, drinking water

agua purificado/agua puro, *(Latin America)* purified water

aguacate, avocado

aguardiente, *(Latin America)* sugar cane or
    corn based liquor

aguja, needlefish/sparkling beverage

agujas, en, on skewers

ahumado, smoked

ahumados variados, smoked fish

ajada, garlic & oil sauce

ajedrea, savory

ajetes, garlic shoots

ají, chili, red pepper

ají de gallina, *(Peru)* shredded chicken in a cream & pepper sauce

ajiaceite, garlic oil/garlic mayonnaise

We drink bottled water as often as we can, for the taste as much as for purity.

Aquardiente, like white lightening, has an extremely high alcohol content.

Peppers & Tomatoes are members of the same family.

29

ajiaco bogotano, *(Columbia)* thick potato soup (frequently w/chicken)

ajilla, garlic sauce

ajillo, cooked in garlic & oil

ajillo moruno, Moorish casserole of bread, almonds, chopped beef or liver, garlic & seasonings

ajo, al, contains whole garlic cloves

ajo, garlic

ajo arriero, with garlic, paprika & parsley

ajo blanco, cold almond & garlic soup

ajo de Mataero, dish of bacon, liver & pork

ajonjolí, sesame seed

ajopollo, chicken w/garlic & almond sauce

al, a la, with/in the style of

aladroc, anchovies

alajú, cake w/honey & almonds

alas, wings

albacora, *(South America)* swordfish

albahaca, basil

albardado, in a batter

albaricoque, apricot

albariño, al, in a white wine sauce

albariño, white wine

albóndigas, meatballs/fishballs

albufera, sauce w/red pepper & cream

alcachofa, artichoke

alcachofas a la andaluza, artichokes w/bacon & ham

alcaparra, caper

alcapurias, *(Puerto Rico)* ground plantains w/fish or meat fried in batter

alcaravea, caraway seed

alcohólica, alcoholic beverage

alfajores, *(Chile)* small round cakes

Ajo

Albacora.

Albóndigas are often served as appetizers.

Alfajores are the national dessert of Chile.

30

algar-robina, *(Peru)* pisco & carob syrup

alicantina, a la, w/green peppers,
artichokes & seafood

aliñada, marinated or seasoned
or w/salad dressing

aliño, dressing

alioli/ali oli/all-i-oli, garlic mayonnaise/garlic purée

allada, garlic & oil sauce

ali-pebre/all-i-pebre, garlic, oil & paprika sauce

almadrote, sauce w/garlic, cheese & eggplant

almejas, clams

almejas a la buena mujer, clams in a wine & parsley sauce

almejas a la marinera, clams in a white sauce

almejas al natural/almejas naturales, live clams

A la buena mujer means of the good woman.

almendrada, cooked w/almonds

almendras, almonds

almendras garrapiñadas, sugar coated toasted almonds

almendras tostadas, toasted almonds

almíbar, syrup

almojábanas, syrup-coated buns.
(Columbia) corn muffins

almuerzo, lunch

aloque, red wine (made from a mixture of
white & red grapes)

alpargata, sweet biscuit

alubias, kidney beans/broad beans/fava beans

Alubias blancas are white beans, rojas are red, rosadas, pink.

amanida, salad w/fish & meat

amargo, bitter

amarilla, en, sauce w/saffron & onions

amarillos (en dulce), *(Puerto Rico)* ripe (yellow) plantains
fried in a red wine, sugar & cinnamon sauce

31

amontillado, medium dry sherry, older than ***jerez fino,*** is aged at least 8 years in wood

anacardos, cashews

anafre, *(Honduras)* bean paste smothered w/melted cheese

ananás, *(Latin America)* pineapples

ancas de rana, frog legs

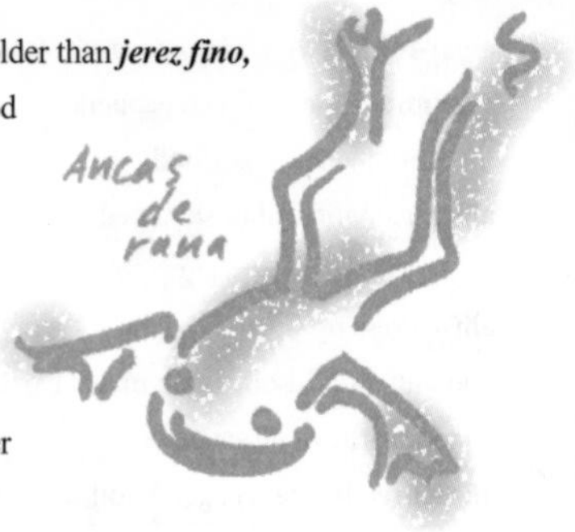
Ancas de rana

ancho, *(Mexico)* dried *poblano* pepper

anchoas, anchovies

anchoas a la barquera, anchovies w/capers

andalucía, dry sherry & orange juice

andaluza, a la, w/red peppers, tomatoes & garlic

añejo, aged

angélica, *(Basque)* liquor similar to yellow Chartreuse

angelote, angelfish

anguilas, eels

anguila

angulas, baby eels

anís, anise/anise flavored liquor

anisado, anise flavored soda

anís seco, anise flavored beverage

añojo, veal

anona, custard apple

The skewered meat of Anticucho is often beef heart.

anticucho, *(Latin America)* beef kebabs

antojito, *(Guatemala)* *tortilla* sandwich filled w/beef, tomatoes & onions. *(Mexico)* this refers to any snack

aperitivo, cocktail/aperitif

api, *(Latin America)* drink made from corn & cinnamon

apio, celery

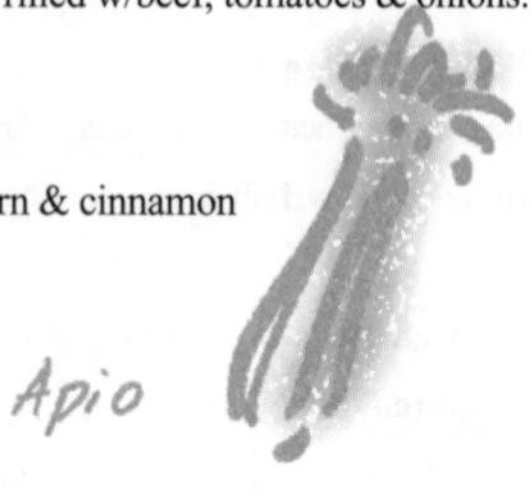
Apio

arandano, cranberry

arencas, salted sardines

arenque, herring

arenque en escabeche, pickled herring

arepa, *(Latin America)* corn meal pancake.

> *(Columbia)* fried breakfast corn muffin. *(Venezuela)* these have a crisp outside & a soft inside & frequently contain cheese

armañac, *(Chile)* a type of brandy made from *aguardiente*

aromáticas, *(Latin America)* herbal teas

Armañac

arrope, honey syrup

arròs, rice dish/soup w/rice. ***Arròs en cassola*** is a dish of rice w/assorted seafood from *Costa Brava*. ***Arròs negre*** is a squid and rice dish from *Catalonia*

arroz, rice

Arroz a la Cubana is sometimes made with banana instead of tomato.

arroz a la banda, fish & rice w/saffron dish

arroz a la catalana, rice w/peppers & sausage

arroz a la Cubana, rice w/tomato sauce & fried egg

arroz a la emperatriz, rice w/apricots, raisins, truffles, milk & Contreau

arroz a la española, rice w/chicken livers, pork, & tomatoes

arroz a la mexicana, *(Mexico)* a blend of tomatoes, rice & onions

arroz a la valenciana, rice w/chicken, vegetables & shellfish

arroz a la vasca, rice w/chicken giblets

Almost everything in the Dominican Republic is served with Rice and beans—

arroz al canario, rice w/ham & bananas

arroz al caldo, consommé w/rice

arroz blanco, boiled, steamed rice

arroz brut, dry soup (see *sopas secas*) of rice & meats

arroz caldoso, rice soup

arroz con cacao, *(Panama)* chocolate flavored rice pudding

arroz con coco y titi, *(Panama)* rice w/coconut & shrimp

Arroz con habichuelas.

arroz con costra, rice *(paella)* w/meatballs

arroz con dulce, *(Puerto Rico)* sweet rice pudding

arroz con habichuelas, *(Dominican Republic, Puerto Rico)* rice & beans

arroz con leche, rice pudding

33

arroz con mariscos, rice w/seafood

arroz con pollo, rice & chicken

arroz empedrat, rice with beans & tomatoes

arroz escarlata, rice w/shrimp & tomatoes

arroz marinera, rice w/assorted seafood

arroz moro, *(Latin America)* rice w/spicy meat

arroz negro, rice made black by cooking in squid ink

arroz primavera, rice w/vegetables

arvejas, *(Latin America)* peas

asadillo, roasted, skinned peppers w/garlic

asado, roasted/roasted meats.

> *(Paraguay)* beef grilled on an open fire.

> *(Uruguay)* barbecued beef

asado de tira, *(Latin America)* spareribs

asadurilla, lamb's liver stew

asopao, *(Puerto Rico, Dominican Republic)* a thick
stew made w/rice & w/meat or seafood

asturias, sharp flavored cheese

ata, whipped cream

atole, *(Latin America)* oat-based beverage

atún, tuna

auyama, *(Venezuela)* a fruit similar to pumpkin

avellana, hazelnuts

avena, oats. Can also refer to oat meal

aves, poultry

azafrán, saffron

azahar, orange blossom

azúcar, sugar

azúcar de acre, maple syrup

azúcar demerara, granulated brown sugar

azúcar enpolvo/azúcar glace, powdered sugar

Arroz moro is a Cuban specialty.

Asopao is Puerto Rico's most popular dish.

atun.

In South America you'll find Ave Tomate Sandwiches. Chicken and Tomato.

34

azúcar moreno, brown sugar

bacalao/balcallao, salt cod

bacalao a la catalana, cod w/ham, parsley, garlic & almonds

bacalao al ajo arriero, cod w/parsley, garlic & peppers

bacalao a la riojana, cod & sauce w/paprika & peppers

bacalao a la vizcaína, cod w/ham, peppers, tomato sauce & potatoes.

(Puerto Rico) cod stewed in a rich tomato sauce

bacalao pil-pil, *(Basque)* cod casserole w/garlic & oil.

(Latin America) cod w/garlic & peppers

bacalitos (fritos), *(Puerto Rico)* fried cod fritters

bacon, bacon

baho, *(Nicaragua)* tomato & beef stew

bajoques farcides, meat & rice stuffed in red peppers

baleadada, *(Latin America) tortilla* filled w/cheese, beans & eggs

bandarillo/banderillo, small skewer with ham, cheese or pickle

bandeja paisa, *(Latin America)* main dish. *(Columbia)* a dish w/ground beef, sausage, salt pork, beans, rice, avocado & fried egg.

This dish is also called ***plato montañero***

barbacoa, barbecued

barbo, barbel (a fresh water fish)

barcoretta, tuna

barra, bar (as in a chocolate bar)

bartolillos, deep fried pastry filled w/custard

batata, sweet potato

batida/batido, milk shake. *(Dominican Republic, Mexico)* fruit milk shake

baveresa de coco, cold coconut dessert

bayas, berries

bebidas, beverages

bebidas alcohólicas, alcoholic beverages

bebidas refrescantes, soft drinks

becada, woodcock

[handwritten note:] Barra de Pan is a loaf of Bread.

[handwritten note:] Batata blanca is sweet potato with pink skin and yellow flesh.

beicon, bacon

berberecho, cockle

berenjena, eggplant/aubergine

berenjenas a la mallorquina, eggplants w/garlic mayonnaise

berraza, parsnip

berros, watercress

bertón, stuffed cabbage

berza, cabbage

besugo, sea bream/porgy

besugo asado con piriñaca, bream baked w/red peppers

besugo mechado, bream stuffed w/bacon & ham

beterragas, sweet potatoes

bicarbonato de sosa, baking soda

bien cocido, well done

bien hecho, well done

bien-me-sabe coco, *(Venezuela)* cake w/coconut cream topping.

> *(Puerto Rico)* sponge cake w/coconut topping

bien pasado, well done

bife, *(Latin America)* steak

bife a lo pobre, *(Chile)* large steak w/fried

> potatoes & onions, served w/two fried eggs on top

bife de lomo, *(Argentina)* T-bone steak served without the bone

biftec, beef steak

biftek de ternera/bistek de ternera, veal steak

biftec encebollado, *(Mexico)* steak w/fried onions

biftek salteado al jerez, fried steak w/sherry

bis/bisso, chub (mackerel)

bistek, beef steak

bizcocho, sponge cake dessert

bizcochos borrachos, sponge cake soaked in liquor (usually rum)

> and/or syrup

Handwritten note: No matter what language you say parsnip in, it doesn't sound good to us.

Handwritten note: Bien me sabe means I know it does me good.

Handwritten note: Bistek — Bien Cocido.

36

bizcotela, cookie

blanco y negro, iced milk, coffee & cinnamon

blando, soft

blanquillos, *(Latin America)* eggs

bocadillo, snack/sandwich usually w/ham & cheese

bocadillos de monja (nun's mouthful), cake w/egg, sugar & almonds

bocas, *(Costa Rica)* small appetizers served w/alcoholic beverages

bodega, wine or sherry cellar

bogovante/bogavante, lobster

boletos, cepe/porcini mushrooms

bolillos, *(Mexico)* sandwich bread rolls

bolitas, cheese balls

bollito, bread roll/bun

bollo, bread roll/bun/breakfast roll baked w/sugar

bollo de panizo, scone made of cornmeal

bollo escocés, scone

bollo preñado, roll filled with meat

bollos de maíz, *(Venezuela)* deep fried corn puffs

bomba, meatball w/chili sauce

bomba helada, baked Alaska

bombón, bonbon

boniato, yam

Bonito are small tuna

bonito, tuna

boquerones, anchovies. A popular first course in *Spain*

boquitas, *(Guatemala)* small appetizers such as olives, peanuts or crackers

Boquitas means little months

bori-bori, *(Paraguay)* chicken soup w/cornmeal balls

borona, cornmeal

borra, cod, spinach & potato soup

borracho, grey gurnard (seafood)

borrachos, cakes soaked in wine or syrup

botella, bottle *Bo tay-yah*

botella media, half bottle *Bo·tay·yah May·dee·ah*

bover, snail

brandada de bacalao, creamy cod purée *bover*

brasa, barbecued/grilled

braseado/a, braised

brazo de gitano, sponge cake roll w/custard filling.

> *(Latin America)* sponge cake w/jam filling

Brazo de gitano means gypsy arm.

breca, a type of sea bream

brécol, broccoli

brevas, deep fried doughnuts w/custard filling.

> *(Latin America)* figs

bróccolis/bróculi, broccoli

brochetas, en, on skewers

broquil, broccoli

brotes, bean sprouts

brut, extremely dry wine

Not the budin found in creole countries which is blood sausage and is called ButiFarra. iN Latin America.

budín, pudding/custard. *(Latin America)* cake

buey, beef

buey de mar, large-clawed crab

buey estofado, beef stew w/potatoes, sausage & wine

buñuelo, fried pastry/doughnut.

> *(Columbia)* baked flour & cheese ball served at breakfast.

> *(Mexico)* deep fried *tortillas* topped w/sugar

buñuelo de bacalao, fried pastry w/dried, salted cod

buñuelo de cuaresma rellenos, fried pastry w/chocolate & cream

buñuelo de viento, *(Panama)* dessert of fried doughnuts w/syrup

bunyettes, doughnuts

burrito, *(Mexico)* stuffed *tortilla*

búsano, whelk (seafood)

buseca, *(Latin America)* spicy oxtail soup. A specialty in *Uruguay*

butifarra, spiced sausage made of pork and/or veal.

   (Latin America) spicy blood sausage

buvangos rellenos, stuffed zucchini

caballa, mackerel

cabello de ángel, stewed sweet

   pumpkin or squash

Cabeza de Cerdo is a fish but the name means Pig's head.

cabeza de cerdo, brawn

cabeza de ternera, seasoned veal loaf/calf's head

cabra, goat. This can also refer to a spider crab in Catalonia

cabracho, scorpion fish

cabrales, a creamy blue, cheese

cabrillo, comber (seafood)

cabrito, goat (kid)

cabrito asado roasted kid is a specialty in *Mexico*

cacao, cocoa

cacahuetes, peanuts

cacereña, black olive

cacerola, casserole

cachelada, potato & sausage stew

cachelos, diced, boiled potato dish

cachito, *(Latin America)* croissant

café, coffee

café americano, *(Mexico)* black coffee

café con agua caliente, coffee w/hot water (to dilute)

café con leche coffee with milk.

   (Columbia) milk is served

   w/a small amount of coffee

café cortado, small cup of coffee

   w/a small amount of milk or cream

café de olla, *(Latin America)* coffee w/cinnamon & sugar

café descafeinado, decaffeinated coffee

café exprés, espresso

café granizado, ice coffee

café guayoyo, *(Venezuela)* large cup of mild, black coffee

café irlandés, Irish coffee

café marrón, *(Venezuela)* a large cup of strong coffee
with a small amount of milk

café marroncito, *(Venezuela)* small cup of strong coffee
with a small amount of milk

café negrito, *(Venezuela)* small cup of strong black coffee

café negro, black coffee

café perfumado, *(Latin America)* coffee w/milk

café perico, *(Columbia)* coffee w/liquor (usually brandy)

café solo, demitasse/black coffee

café tinto, *(Columbia)* black coffee

café vienés, black coffee & whipped cream

caguama, *(Latin America)* turtle

cailón, shark

caimito, *(Puerto Rico)* star shaped apple

calabacín (or calabacita), zucchini

calabaza, pumpkin. *(Dominican Republic)* a squash side dish

calamares, squid

calamares en su tinta, squid in onion, tomato & squid ink sauce

calamares fritos, deep fried squid

calcots, spring onions

calda/caldo, hot

caldeirada, stew. *(Latin America)* fish stew

caldera de dátiles de mar, seafood stew

caldereta, stew/casserole

caldereta asturiana, seafood stew

Cafe Irlandés

you may want to make sure you're not eating an endangered species.

caguama.

calamares.

40

caldereta de cordero a la pastora, lamb & vegetable stew

caldereta de gallega, vegetable stew

caldero, cauldron

caldillo, clear fish soup

caldillo de congrio, *(Chile)* conger eel soup w/potatoes & tomatoes

caldillo de perro, hake soup

caldo/calda, hot

caldo, broth/consommé

caldo de, soup

Caldo means hot temperature, Caliente, spicy hot.

caldo de gallina, chicken soup

caldo de pescado, fish soup

caldo de res, *(Mexico)* beef stock & vegetable soup

caldo gallego, meat & vegetable soup (frequently ham & cabbage)

caldo guanche, soup w/potatoes, tomatoes, onions, & zucchini

caldo verde, cabbage-based broth w/potato & greens

caliente, hot. Often refers to a dish w/a hot chili sauce

callampas, *(Chile)* mushrooms

callos, tripe

callos a la catalana, tripe stew w/wine & pine nuts

callampas.

callos a la madrileña, tripe stew w/peppers, sausage, ham & tomatoes.

   (Latin America) tripe stew w/peppers

camarera, waitress

camarero, waiter

Camarones.

camarones, shrimp

camarones a la plancha, *(Mexico)* shrimp marinated & then grilled

camarones del rio, freshwater crayfish

camote, *(Bolivia)* sweet potato

caña, *(Paraguay)* alcoholic beverage made from sugar cane & similar to rum.

   (Spain) a large mug of draft beer

caña de dulce, sugar cane

caña de vaca, marrow bone

cañadilla/cañailla, snail

canela, cinnamon

canelones, cannelloni

canelones a la barcelonesa, ham & chicken liver stuffed cannelloni

cangrejo (de mar), crab

cangrejo (de río), crayfish (river crab)

canilla, snack

cantarela, chanterelle mushroom

capirotada, meat dish in an almond sauce

capitán, *(Peru) pisco* & vermouth

capitón, grey mullet

caqui, persimmon

carabineros, large shrimp

caracoles, snails

carajillo, coffee w/brandy

carajillo de ron, coffee w/rum

carajillo de vodka, coffee w/vodka

carajitos, hazelnut macaroons

carambola, starfruit

caramelo, caramel. *(Latin America)* dessert

caraotas, *(Latin America)* beans

carbón, *(Mexico)* any charcoal grilled filling

carbonada, *(Argentina)* beef stew, usually w/rice, sweet potatoes, squash, apples & peaches (baked in a pumpkin shell) also called **carbonada criollo**. *(Uruguay)* meat & rice stew w/peas, peaches & raisins

carbonada de buey, beef cooked in beer

carbonero, coalfish, coley or saithe

cardamomo, cardamom

cardo, cardoon

Handwritten annotations:

Many European dishes, like cannelloni, find themselves on the menus of South and Central America, their names — and sometimes their recipes — slightly altered.

cantarella.

Carojillo can also be served with Anisette.

Carbonada is the Argentine version of Belgian Carbonade.

42

cargol, snail

cargol.

cari, curry

carimañolas, *(Panama)* turnover filled w/cheese or meat

carne, meat

carne a la parilla, grilled steak

carne alambres, *(Mexico)* meat on a skewer

carne asada, grilled meat/barbecued beef

carne asada a la tampiqueña, *(Mexico)* beefsteak w/guacamole and beans

carne asada al horno, roast meat

carne de caza, game

carne de cerdo, pork

carne de chancho, *(Latin America)* pork

carne de lidia, very tough beef

carne de mebrillo, quince jelly

carne de res, beef

carne de res con chile colorado, *(Mexico)* beef in red chile

carne de vaca, beef

carne en salsa, meat in tomato sauce

carne guisada, *(Guatemala)* sauce w/stewed beef

carne mechada, *(Dominican Republic, Puerto Rico)* a beef roast served
    w/onions, ham & spices

carne molida, ground beef

carne para asar, beef roast

carne picada, ground meat

carnero, mutton

carnero verde, mutton dish w/parsley & mint

carnitas, *(Latin America)* barbecued pork

carpa.

carpa, carp

carquinyolis, almond biscuit

carrillada, pig cheek

carro de queso, *(Latin America)* cheese platter

carta, la, menu

Camarero, una carta por favor!

carta de vinos, wine list

cártamo, safflower

casa, de la, of the house, could mean *specialty* or *home made*

casadiellas, dessert turnovers

casados, *(Costa Rica)* fish, meat or chicken w/rice, beans & vegetables

cáscara, rind/zest/peel/shell

casero, homemade

casi crudo, very rare

castañas, chestnuts

castellana, bread & garlic soup

castoñola, sea perch

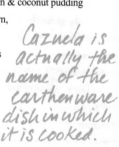

castoñola

catalana, a la, cooked in a tomato sauce

causa a la limeña, *(Peru)* potato pureé w/shrimp salad

cava, sparkling wine

caza, game

cazadora, a la, w/mushrooms, onions & herbs

a la cazadora.

cazón, dogfish/shark

cazón en adobo, floured & deep fried shark marinated
in vinegar, paprika, cumin & oregano

cazuela, stew/casseroled. *(Puerto Rico)* pumpkin & coconut pudding

cazuela de ave, *(Chile)* casserole w/beans, corn,
rice, pumpkin, carrots & spices

Cazuela is actually the name of the earthenware dish in which it is cooked.

cazuela de cordero, lamb stew w/vegetables

cazuela de chichas, meat casserole

cebada, barley

cebiche, see *ceviche*

cebolla, onion

cebolletas, scallions/chives

cebollinos, chives

cebrero, a creamy blue cheese

44

cecina, beef jerky/strip steak

cena, dinner/supper

cenicero, ashtray

centeno, rye bread

centollo, spider crab. *(Chile)* king crab

centollo relleno, spider crab cooked in its shell

cepa, wine grape

cerdo, pork

cereales, cereals

cerezas, cherries

cerveza, beer

cerveza de barril, draft beer

cerveza dorada, light (in color, not necessarily in calories) beer

cerveza extranjera, imported beer

cerveza negra, dark beer

césar/ensalada césar, Caesar salad

cesta de frutas, selection of fruit

Cerveza nationale is domestic beer and cerveza importada is imported beer. In case you couldn't figure that out.

cesta de frutas

ceviche, seafood marinated in lemon & lime juice frequently served as an appetizer of raw seafood.

(Peru) raw seafood marinated in lemon juice & hot peppers.

(Mexico & Latin America) raw seafood salad which frequently contains *jalapeños*, onions, cilantro & diced tomatoes.

(Dominican Republic, Puerto Rico) raw fish is marinated in peppers (hot and bell), cilantro, onions, vegetables & herbs and often served as a salad

chabacano, apricot

chabacano.

chacina, ground sausage

chacoli, Basque white wine

chairo, *(Bolivia)* lamb broth w/*chuños* & vegetables

chajá, *(Uruguay)* sponge cake, cream & jam dessert

45

chalote, chalotas, shallots

chalupa, *(Mexico)* deep fried *tortilla* w/many fillings

champaña/champán, champagne

champiñon, mushroom

chancho, *(Latin America)* pork

chanfaina, pig stew w/rice & blood sausage stew

chanfaina castellana, rice & sheeps' liver stew

changurro, spider crab

chanquetes, deep fried small fish similar to whitebait

chapin, *(Puerto Rico)* trunkfish

chato, glass of red wine

chauchas, *(Latin America)* green beans

chayote, *(Latin America)* pear-shaped vegetable similar to squash

cherna, grouper

chica, *(Chile)* alcoholic beverage of fermented grapes & juice

chica de jora, *(Peru)* alcoholic beverage made from corn.

The non-alcoholic version is ***chica morada***

chica de manzana, apple brandy

chicha, *(Bolivia)* an alcoholic beverage made from corn

chicharos, *(Latin America)* peas

chicharro, mackerel

chicharrones, pork fat/fried pork rinds/fried pork skin

chicharrones de pollo, *(Dominican Republic, Peru)* crispy fried chicken pieces

chichicuilotes, *(Mexico)* small sparrows boiled live
served stuffed w/avocado

chico zapote, *(Mexico)* the tropical fruit sapodilla

chifa, *(Latin America)* Chinese food

chilaquiles, *(Mexico)* pieces of fried *tortillas*
w/onions, red peppers,
cheese & sour cream

chilcano, *(Peru)* pisco & ginger ale

Handwritten margin notes:

Chalupa, which actually means boat, is named for the boat shape of the finished tortilla.

chicharos.

You may want to avoid this dish considering its grim preparation method.

chile, chili pepper. Sweet to horribly hot & all shapes & colors! The Scoville scale ranks the fire power of a chili pepper. The hottest is a *habanero* w/a measure of 100,000 to 300,000 units. In comparison, a *jalapeño* has a rank of 2500-5000 units

chiles.

chile poblano, *(Mexico)* green pepper

chiles en nogada, green peppers stuffed w/whipped cream & nut sauce

chiles rellenos, stuffed peppers.

(Mexico) they are coated w/batter & fried

chili, chili

chilindrón, refers to the use of red peppers & tomatoes in a dish.

For example, ***pollo chilindrón*** is a dish of chicken w/red peppers

chillo, *(Dominican Republic, Puerto Rico)* red snapper

chimichanga, *(Mexico)* deep fried *tortilla* stuffed w/beef, beans & chilies

chimichurri, *(Argentina)* barbecue sauce of tomatoes, garlic, onions

china, *(Dominican Republic, Puerto Rico)* a sweet orange

chinola, *(Dominican Republic)* passion fruit

chipas, *(Paraguay)* bread made of corn flour, cheese & eggs

chipi chipi, *(Venezuela)* clam soup

chipiron.

chipirón, small squid

chipotle, *(Latin America)* dark chili sauce/a smoked *jalapeño* pepper

chiquito, glass of red wine   *chiquito!*

chirimoyas, custard apple.

(Ecuador) a custard apple jungle fruit

chirivias, parsnips   *The less said about parsnips ...*

chirmol, *(Latin America)* hot sauce made of onions, tomatoes & mint.

(Guatemala) grilled steak w/tomato & onion sauce

chistorra, a narrow sausage

chivito, *(Uruguay)* steak sandwich

chivito al plato, *(Uruguay)* steak topped w/a fried egg & served w/potato salad, a green salad & french fries

chivo, goat, kid

choclo, pastel de, *(Chile)* a corn casserole filled w/a variety of meats & vegetables. This can also refer to corn on the cob

chocolate, chocolate

chocolate caliente, hot chocolate.

> *Chocolate a la española* is a thick hot chocolate drink

chocolate con leche, hot chocolate milk

chocolate santafereño, *(Bolivia)* hot chocolate & cheese

chocolatina, chocolate bar/candy bar

chocos, large squid/cuttlefish

cholga, *(Chile)* giant mussels

chongos, *(Latin America)* cheese in a sweet syrup

chop, *(Chile)* beer (usually draft beer)

chopa, a type of sea bream

chopitos, cuttlefish

choricero, chili

choripán, *(Uruguay)* sausage baked in dough

choritos, small mussels

chorizo, cured sausage seasoned w/paprika & garlic, almost always pork sausage. In *Mexico*, the sausage is usually made from *fresh* ground pork

choros, mussels

choto, baby goat. *Choto ajillo* is kid in a garlic casserole

chuchitos, *(Guatemala)* meat & sauce in dough & wrapped in a corn husk

chuchuco, *(Columbia)* barley, meat & peppercorn soup

chucrut, sauerkraut

chufa, tiger nut

Handwritten margin notes:

chocolate is native to South America.

Hot chocolate and chocolate drinks are ubiQuitous in Latin America.

¿chocolate caliente.

During the InQuisition, a chorizo hung in the Kitchen indicated that a christian lived there.

48

chufle, *(Bolivia)* an alcoholic beverage
made w/*singani*, lemon juice & soda

chuleta, cutlet/chop

chuleta de gamo, venison

chuletita/chuletilla, small cutlet/small chop

chuletón, rib beef chop/large chop

chumbera/chumbo, prickly pear

chuños, *(Bolivia, Peru)* freeze dried potatoes
(frequently mixed w/meat, eggs or fish)

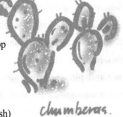

chumberas.

chupe de camarones, *(Peru)* shrimp stew.
Chupe de mariscos is seafood stew

chupete, *(Latin America)* sucker/lollipop

churisco, *(Latin America)* baked sausage

churrasco, *(Argentina, Uruguay)* grilled steak (usually a thin slice).
(Ecuador) fried beef w/rice, potatoes, vegetables, avocado, & fried egg

churros, extremely popular fried breakfast pastry

cidra, squash/squash boiled in sugar

cidracayote de verano, summer squash

cierva, deer

cigalas, prawns

cigalas cocidas, boiled prawns (sometimes lobster)

cigarra de mer, (clawless) lobster

cilantro, cilantro/coriander.
This herb is used heavily in *Mexico*

cilantro.

cincho, hard cheese made from sheeps' milk

ciruela, plum

ciruelas pasas/ciruelas secas, prunes

civet de liebre, marinated rabbit

clara, beverage made from a mixture of beer & lemonade

clara de huevo, egg white

clarete, light red wine/rosé wine

claro, light (in color)

clavo, clove

clementina, mandarin orange

clérico, *(Latin America)* wine & fruit juice

clima, al, at room temperature

coca, pie

coca amb pinxes, sardine pie

coca mallorquina, similar to a pizza

cocadas/cocados, coconut cakes.
  (Mexico) coconut cooked w/sugar, egg yolks & sherry

cocarois, similar to a pizza & topped w/raisins & pine nuts

cochifrito, milk fed lamb stew

cochifrito de cordero, highly seasoned lamb stew

cochinillo, suckling pig

cochinillo asado, roasted suckling pig

cochinita, chopped pork dish

cocido, cooked, boiled, simmered

cocido al vapor, steamed

cocido envuelto, baked in parchment

cocido castellano, thick stew w/sausage,
    chickpeas, chicken, bacon,
    potatoes & other vegetables

cocido con leche, *(Paraguay)* maté w/milk

cocido madrileño, (Madrid stew) stew made from meat,
    vegetables & chickpeas

cocina casera, home cooking

coco, coconut

coco loco, *(Mexico)* coconut flavored alcoholic beverage

cocoa, chocolate

cococas, pieces of hake gills. See *kokoxas*

cocos, coconut cakes

Coca Mallorquina and Cocarois are specialties of the Balearic Islands, off the Southern coast of Spain.

cochinello

cocos frios, *(Dominican Republic, Puerto Rico)* chilled coconuts, tops chopped off, drunk with a straw *With or without rum, cocos frios are called the same thing.*

cóctel, cocktail

cóctel campechana marinera, *(Mexico)* oyster & shrimp cocktail

cóctel de camarón, shrimp cocktail

cóctel de mariscos, seafood cocktail

codillo de cerdo, pigs' feet

codoñate, quince, chestnut & honey cake

codoñate de nueces, walnut cake

codorniz (codornices), quail

cogollo de palmito, hearts of palm

cohombro, cucumber

col, cabbage

col de Bruselas, Brussels sprout

cola, tail

cola de mono, coffee, rum, milk & *pisco*. *(Chile) aguardiente,* coffee, sugar, milk, cinnamon & egg yolk. Similar to egg nog

colecillas de Bruselas, *(Latin America)* Brussels sprouts

coles, cabbage leaves

coliflor, cauliflower

coliflor con bechamel, cauliflower & cheese

collejas, corn salad

colmenilla, morel mushrooms

comida, lunch/meal

comida corrida, is a fixed price menu in *Mexico* & *comida corriente* is a fixed priced menu in *Central America*

comino, cumin (used in Mexican chili powders)

compota, compote/stewed fruit

completo, hot dog

con, with. Often, this is abbreviated as *c/*

Cocos frios.

Cohombro.

Cola de Mono means Monkey Tail.

Completo.

con hielo, beverage served "on the rocks"

coñac, brandy/cognac

concentrado, concentrate.

    Concentrado de tomate is tomato paste

CONAC.

concha, conch

conchas finas, large scallops/Venus clam

conchas peregrinas, scallops

conchitas, *(Peru)* scallops

condimentos, condiments/seasonings

conejo, rabbit

conchas finas.

conejo del monte, wild rabbit

confitura, jam

congrio, conger eel

conserva, pickled

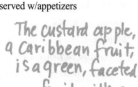

congrio

consomé/consumado, clear soup (frequently chicken broth)

consomé a la reina, consommé w/egg

consomé de chivo, *(Mexico)* goat soup

contra de ternera, veal stew

contrafilete de ternera, veal fillet

copa, glass

copa de helado, assorted ice cream served in a glass

copa nuria, egg whipped & served w/jam

copetin, *(Uruguay)* any alcoholic beverage served w/appetizers

copitas, sherry glass

coques/coquetes, flat bread

    frequently used for pizza dough

coquinas, clams

coquito, *(Puerto Rico)* holiday coconut eggnog w/rum

corazón, heart/core. *(Puerto Rico)* custard apple

corazón de alcachofa, artichoke heart

corazón de palma, hearts of palm

The custard apple, a Caribbean fruit, is a green, faceted fruit with a delicate taste and soft, sweet flesh.

corazonada, hearts stewed in sauce

cordero, lamb

cordero al chilindrón, lamb w/red peppers

cordero lechal asado, roast lamb

cordero mamón, suckling lamb

cordero recental, spring lamb

cortadillo, small pancake w/lemon

corto, glass of draft beer

corvina, white sea bass

corzo, deer

cosecha, vintage. *Cosechero* is the latest vintage of red wine

costada, flank

costellada, grilled lamb chops

costilla, chop/spareribs

costilla de cerdo con poco carne, spareribs

costra, crust

costrada, slice of cake or pastry

costrada navarra, thick soup topped w/a bread crust

cranc verd, shore crab

crema, cream, mousse, or purée (soup).

Can refer to sour cream in *Mexico*

crema batida, whipped cream

crema catalana, crème caramel

cremada, dessert made from sugar, milk & eggs

crema de arroz, creamy rice pudding

crema de cacao, chocolate liquor

crema de café, coffee liquor

crema de maranja, Curacao

crema de menta, créme de menthe

crema de San José, chilled custard

crema española, milk, eggs & fruit jelly dessert

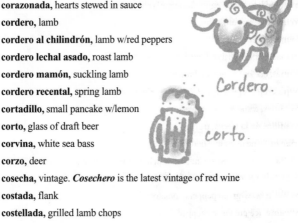

Cordero.

corto.

vela de cumpleaños

Costrada chocolaTe.

Créme Caramel, also called flan, is popular in all Spanish speaking countries.

53

crema nieve, frothy egg-yolk, sugar, rum or wine

cremadina, custard filling

cremas, sweet liquors

cremat, coffee w/rum & brandy

cremat, cooked to golden brown

crepa/crep/crepe, crêpe. *Crepe imperial* is crêpe suzette

criadillas, testicles/sweetbreads *Thanks, but No thanks.*

criadillas de la tierra, truffles

crianza, wine aged in wood barrels

criolla, *(Puerto Rico)* island cuisine which blends European, African, Taino & Arawak Indian foods *That's Creole to us.*

criolla, a la, w/green peppers, tomatoes & spices

crocante, ice cream w/chopped nuts

croquetas, fish or meat dumplings. *(Paraguay)* breaded & deep fried pieces of chicken, pork or beef

cru de peix, fish stew which contains raw or slightly cooked fish

crudo, raw

cuajada, creme-based dessert w/honey

cuarto, roast/joint

cubalibre, rum & coca-cola

cubana, a la, w/eggs & fried bananas

Cuba Libre.

cubano, *(Puerto Rico)* sandwich made of ham, chicken and/or pork, Swiss cheese, mustard & pickles

cubata, cocktail mixed w/a soft drink

cubierto, cover charge

cubito de hielo, ice cube

cubra libre, rum & coca-cola. *(Spain)* sometimes this is gin & coca cola

cucaracha, *tequila* & coffee flavored alcoholic beverage

cuchara, spoon

cuchifrito, *(Dominican Republic, Puerto Rico)* a stew of pork innards

cuchillo, knife

cuello, neck

cuenta, la, check/bill

cuerpo, de, full-bodied beverage

cuitlacoche, *(Latin America)* a type of mushroom

culantro, cilantro/coriander

curanto, *(Chile)* dish of meat (often suckling pig),
    vegetables & seafood

curí, *(Columbia)* grilled guinea pig

cusuco, *(Latin America)* armadillo

cuy, *(Columbia)* grilled guinea pig

damasco, apricot

dátil, date

dátiles de mar, shellfish

delicias, small sponge cake

delicias de queso, breaded & deep fried cheese

dentón, dentex (a type of bream)

desayuno, breakfast

descafeinado, decaffeinated

despojos, innards (offal)

destornillador, "screwdriver" vodka & orange juice

día, del, "of the day"

diente de ajo, clove of garlic

donastiarra, a la, charcoal grilled

dorada, sea bream/dolphin

duelos y quebrantos, scrambled eggs, ham & sausage

dulce, sweet/sweet wine

dulce de batata, *(Argentina)* thick slices of sweet potatoes

dulce de leche, *(Argentina, Uruguay)* milk simmered w/vanilla
    & sugar & served over toast or *flan*

dulce de membrillo, *(Uruguay)* quince preserve

dulce de naranja, marmalade

Handwritten margin notes:

Cuitlacoche, also Huitlacoche is a fungus that grows on corn.

Curí? Thanks but we'll pass. Pass on the cusuco, too.

desayuno en la mañana.

Dorada means golden.

duquesa, a type of fish or vegetable pie

durazno, peach

eglefino, haddock

ejotes, *(Latin America)* pole beans

elotes, *(Latin America)* corn on the cob

emborrachada, marinated (means "drunk")

embuchado, stuffed w/meat

embutido, fresh sausage

embutido de la tierra, local sausage

empanada (empanadas/os), turnover filled w/various ingredients
(breaded & fried). *(Columbia)* they are almost always filled w/potatoes

empanada de gallega, turnover filled w/*chorizo*,
chicken, ham, peppers & onions

empanada de horno, dough filled w/ground meat/ravioli

empanada de lomo, pork & pepper turnover

empanada de pascua, lamb turnover

empanada de vieiras, scallop turnover

empanada salteña, *(Bolivia)* ground meat w/pepper, hot sauce, chicken,
diced potatoes, olives & raisins wrapped in baked dough

empanada santiaguesa, fish turnover or pie

empanadilla, fish or meat patty. *Empanizada* means breaded

emparador/emperador, swordfish

emparedado, hot sandwich

empedrada, salt cod & bean salad

encebollada, in an onion sauce/steak smothered in onions

enchilada, *(Mexico, Latin America)* cheese, chicken or meat filled *tortillas*
topped w/sauce. *Enchiladas & tacos* are both made of *tortillas* rolled
around the fillings. The difference is an *enchilada* is baked w/sauce
over it & a *taco* is served w/the sauce on the side

enchilada Oaxaqueña, *(Mexico)* Oaxaca style *enchilada* w/sliced
chiles poblanos, sour cream, grated cheese & sauce

durazno.

enchilada roja, sausage filled *tortilla*

enchilada suiza, *(Mexico)* stuffed corn *tortillas* topped w/*tomatillo* sauce

enchilada verde, meat or poultry filled *tortilla* dipped in

green tomato sauce

encurtido, pickle

endibia/endivia, chickory/endive

endrinas, blueberries

enebro, juniper berry

eneldo, dill

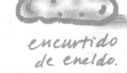

*encurtido
de eneldo.*

pulpo.

ensaimada, breakfast sweet roll (A Mallorcan specialty)

ensalada, salad/rice salad

ensalada a la catalana, cod & white bean salad

ensalada común, green salad

ensalada de frutas, fruit salad

ensalada de habas, cooked bean salad

ensalada de pepinos, cucumber salad

ensalada de pulpo, octopus salad.

A specialty in *Dominican Republic & Puerto Rico*

ensalada de San Isidro, tuna & lettuce salad

ensalada del tiempo, seasonal salad

ensalada ilustrada, mixed salad

ensalada mixta, mixed salad

ensalada simple, green salad

ensalada valenciana, salad w/lettuce, green peppers & oranges

ensalada verde, green salad

ensaladilla rusa, Russian salad

(cold diced potatoes & vegetables w/mayonnaise)

entrada, *(Bolivia)* appetizers, usually tuna, lettuce,

ham and/or hard boiled eggs

entrantes, starters/entrées

entrecot, entrecôte steak/filet mignon

entremés,entremeses, appetizers

entremeses variados, assorted *hors-d'oeuvres*

epazote, *(Mexico)* tea made from an aromatic herb

erizo de mar, sea urchin. *(Chile) erizos* is a dish of raw sea urchins
w/pepper, salt, oil, onion & parsley. Frequently the sea urchin
has a small crab attached to it. Eaten live!

escabeche, pickled/marinated. *(Peru)* cooked fish
appetizer served w/onions &
peppers (served cold). *(Mexico)* fried fish
or shellfish served in a spicy sauce.
(Dominican Republic, Puerto Rico) frying and
then pickling fish to be served hot or cold

arenque en escabeche is pickled herring.

escaldums, poultry fried in onion & tomato sauce

escalfado, poached

escalibada, cod & vegetable salad

escalibada or escalivada, eggplant salad

escaloña, shallot

escalope de ternera, veal scallop

escarcho, red gurnard

escarola, chickory/endive

escocés, scotch

escocés con hielo.

escorpena/escorpión, scorpion

espada/espaldilla, swordfish

espadin, sprat/whitebait

espaguetis italiana, spaghetti

espalda, shoulder

aspárrago

esparragados, scrambled eggs and wild asparagus

espárrago, asparagus

espárragos amargueros, wild asparagus

espárragos calientes, asparagus w/béchamel sauce

espárragos dos salsas, asparagus w/mayonnaise & vinagrette

espárragos trigueros, wild asparagus

especialidad, special

especialidad de la casa, house specialty/chef's specialty

especias, spices

espeto, cooked on a spit

espina, fish bone

espinaca, spinach

espinazo, ribs

espinas.

espuma de jamón, ham mousse

espuma de mar, *(Uruguay)* angel cake w/whipped cream

espumoso, sparkling wine or beverage

esqueixada, red pepper, tomato & cod salad

estacíon, in season

estilo de, in the style of

Estofado & Fabada are favorite meals of ours.

estofado, stewed/braised. *Estofados* means stews

estornino, mackerel (chub)

estragón, tarragon

faba, beans grown between rows of olive trees in *Spain*.
Faves (the plural of *fava*) are dried for use in
winter & eaten fresh in summer. Large & flat,
they can be brown, beige or green.

faves.

Faves are an important part of Spanish
cuisine, especially in Catalonia,
along the Mediterranean

fabada asturiana, pork, beans, sausage & bacon stew

fabes a la Catalana, stew w/beans & black pudding

fabes a la granja, white bean dish

fabricacion casera, homemade

faisán, pheasant

faisán.

faisán a las uvas, pheasant & grapes cooked in port

faisán al modo de Alcántara, pheasant w/port & truffles

faisán de Alcantara, pheasant in Madeira wine sauce

fajitas, really a "Tex-Mex" dish of grilled strips
of meat or shrimp served on a sizzling
plate and eaten w/*tortillas*

falda rellena, stuffed flank

faramallas, sweet fritter

farinato, fried sausage

farro, vegetable soup w/barley

faves, see *fava* above

fesol, dried bean

fiambre, *(Guatemala)* meat, fish & cheese salad

fiambre de bonito, tuna

fiambre de paleta, ham made of shoulder

fiambres, cold cuts

fideos, noodles

fideuà, noodle *paella*/baked noodle dish

filete, fillet (fish or steak). *Filete mignón* is filet mignon

filete de lenguado, fillet of sole

filete de lomo, tenderloin

filete de res, beef steak

filloas, filled crêpes

fino, pale, dry sherry

Argentina raises some of the best beef in the world.

flamenca, a la, w/sausage, green peppers, tomatoes, onions & peas

flamenquines, ham and/or cheese rolled into bread & then fried

flan, caramel custard dessert

flan de café, coffee flavored caramel custard

flaó, cheesecake

flauta, *(Mexico)* filled and deep fried *tortilla* topped w/sauce

flor de calabaza, *(Latin America)* pumpkin flower

flores, flower shaped fritter

fondo de alcachofas, artichoke heart

flauta means flute.

60

frambuesa, raspberry

francesa, a la, in a white sauce/sautéed in butter

fresas, strawberries

fresas de bosque, wild strawberries

fresco, chilled/fresh. *(Central America)* fruit juice

fresón, large strawberry

fresas.

fricadelas, patty of meat

fricandó, fried beef or veal

fricasé, *(Dominican Republic, Puerto Rico)* a stewed chicken dish

   (can also contain stewed goat or rabbit)

fricassé, *(Bolivia)* pork cooked in a spicy sauce &

   served w/potatoes & corn

frijoles, beans (kidney or red beans)

frijoles negros, black beans

frijoles refritos, (refried beans) beans mashed & fried

Black bean Soup is popular in the Caribbean.

frío/fría, cold

fritada, *(Latin America)* fried pieces of meat

fritanga al modo alicante, tuna, fried peppers & garlic

frite, lamb fried w/paprika.

   A specialty in the Spanish region of *Extremadura*

fritillas, rolls (frequently *fritillas al moro*, pork chunks

   wrapped in bacon & served on a toothpick)

frito, fried.

   This can also refer to a dish of fried offal & vegetables

frito de patata, deep fried potato

fritos con jamón, *(Latin America)* fried eggs & ham

fritos de la casa, fried appetizers

fritura, fry. *Frituras,* fried bread

fritura (mixta) de pescado, fried mixed fish

frixuelos, pancakes w/honey

fruta, fruit

huevos fritos.

fruta de Aragón, chocolate coated fruit

fruta escarchada, candied fruit (crystallized fruit)

frutillas, *(Latin America)* strawberries

fuerte, extremely spicy

fundido, fondue

gachas, porridge

gachas manchegas, sweet porridge

galletas, crackers/cookies/biscuits/bread rolls

galletas de nata, sandwich cookies

gallina, chicken

gallina a la cairatraca, chicken stew

gallina de guinea, guinea hen

gallina en pepitoria, chicken stew w/almonds &/or peppers

gallineta, Norway haddock

gallo, rooster

gallo, flatfish

gallo en chica, *(El Salvador)* rooster

gallo pinto, *(Costa Rica)* The national breakfast of
Costa Rica. Mixed cooked beans & rice.
Also found everywhere in *Nicaragua*

gallos, *(Latin America)* tortilla filled w/meat & sauce

galludo, small shark

galupe, grey mullet

gambas, shrimp/prawns

gambas a la americana, shrimp w/garlic & brandy

gambas a la plancha, grilled shrimp (in the shell)

gambas al pil-pil, shrimp w/oil, garlic & hot peppers.
Served on toothpicks, this is a popular *tapa*

gambas con gardinas, battered, deep fried shrimp

gambas con mayonesa, shrimp cocktail

gambas en garbardina, shrimp cooked in batter

fuerte can also mean rich. Literally it means strong.

gallina.

gallo.

gallo pinto means painted rooster.

62

gambas grandes, prawns

gandinga, *(Dominican Republic, Puerto Rico)* spicy kidneys, hearts & livers

gandules, *(Puerto Rico)* pigeon peas

ganso, goose

ganso.

garbanzos, chickpeas

garbanzos a la catalana, chickpeas w/sausage & pine nuts

garbanzos con espinacas, chickpea, spinach & garlic stew

garbure navarro, pork, vegetable & sausage soup

garobo, *(Latin America)* iguana

garrapiñadas, glazed

You can put garobo on the list with curl and cusoco.

gaseoso, drink with carbonation

gâteau basque, filled sweet pastry

gazpacho (andaluz), purée of tomatoes, vinegar, onions, green peppers, garlic, cucumbers & bread crumbs (chilled)

gazpacho was originally a peasant dish made of leftovers.

gazpacho blanco, creamy, white *gazpacho* w/almonds

gazpacho extremeño, white *gazpacho*

gazpacho malagueño, white *gazpacho* w/grapes

gazpacho manchego, pâté of mixed game or stew of game, meat or poultry & vegetables & thickened w/unleavened bread

gazpachuelo, soup w/potatoes, mayonnaise & vinegar

gelatina, jello

jello - you just can't get away from it.

gelats, sorbet

germen de trigo, ground duram wheat

ginebra, gin

girasol.

girasol, sunflower

gitanilla, a la, w/garlic

glorias, small sweet pastry

gol, *(Chile)* alcoholic beverage made of milk, butter & sugar

gordal, large, green olive

gorditas, *(Mexico)* small, thick *tortillas* fried w/chopped meat, cheese,
   beans, vegetables, shredded lettuce & chili sauce on top

gordo, fat/fatty

gorditas–deliciosas!!

gracias, thank you

gran reserva, matured wine

granada, pomegranate

granadina, pomegranate syrup mixed w/wine or brandy

grande, large

granizado, fruit sorbet/crushed ice drink w/fruit syrup or sweetened coffee

granos de maíz, *(Latin America)* sweet corn

granvas, sparkling wine

granvas.

gratén/gratín/gratinado, au gratin

greixera, casserole

greixonera de brossat, cheesecake made from cottage cheese

grelos, turnips/greens

grenadina, grenadine

grillado, *(Latin America)* boneless (for example, *pollo grillado* is boneless
   chicken)

grosella, currant

grosella espinosa, gooseberry

grosella negra.

grosella negra, blackberry

grosella roja, red currant

guacamole, avocado purée. *(Mexico)* dip of mashed avocado, tomato,
   onion, cilantro & chilies

guanabana, *(Dominican Republic, Puerto Rico, Latin America)* custard apple

guandú, *(Panama)* pigeon peas (beans)

guarapo, *(Latin America)* potent alcoholic beverage made from sugar cane

guarnición, garnish

guasacaca, *(Venezuela)* relish of tomatoes, lime juice, onions, avocado

guayaba, guava. *Pasta de guayaba* is guava paste

guayoyo, *(Venezuela)* large cup of mild, black coffee

guinda, a sour black cherry

guindada, *(Latin America)* cherry brandy

guindilla, small, hot pepper/hot pepper sauce.

(Latin America) cherry brandy

guineo, *(Puerto Rico)* banana

guineitos verdes en escabeche, *(Puerto Rico)* pickled green plantains

guirlache, almond & anise candy similar to toffee

guisado, casserole/stew/cooked dish

guisantes, peas

guisantes.

guiso, stew/soup

guiso de maíz, *(Costa Rica)* thick corn stew

guiso de trigo, turnip soup

These grubs show up in bottles of mescal & tequila.

gusanos de maguey, *(Mexico)* fried white grubs

habanero, *(Mexico)* watch out!

The hottest of all peppers

habas, beans. *Habas con jamón* is a casserole of ham and beans

habichuela, bean

habichuela (verde), green bean

hallacas, *(Columbia, Venezuela)* meat & any number of ingredients & spices

stuffed in dough & wrapped in banana leaves & boiled in water

hamburguesa, hamburger

harina, flour

harina de maíz, cornmeal

helado, ice cream

helado de mantecado, custard ice cream

hamburguesa.

helado de nata, custard ice cream

helado de sobores variadas, mixed ice cream

helado quemado, bowl of ice cream topped w/grilled sugar

helote, *(Mexico)* sweet corn pudding ice cream

hervido, boiled, poached.

(Venezuela) soup of vegetables, spices & meat

hielo, ice

hielo, con, a drink "on the rocks"

hierba, herb

hielo.

hierba buena, mint

hierba finas, chopped mixed herbs

hierba luisa, lemon flavored herbal tea

higadillos, chicken livers

hígado, liver

higado de ternera, calf's liver

hígado encebollado, liver & onions

higiditos, chicken livers

higos, figs. *Higos secos* are dried figs

higos a la Malagueña, figs, Málaga style.

figs - relatively uncommon in most of the United States, are ubiquitous in Spain, South and Central America, eaten raw, dried and prepared

A Spanish specialty of sliced figs, wine & sugar

hinojo, fennel

hojaldre, flaky or puff pastry

hojas de laurel, bay leaves

hojas de parra, vine leaves

hojiblanca, black olive

holandas, grape spirit

hongos, mushrooms

horchata, iced, creamy drink made w/honey & almonds.

Sometimes made w/tiny crushed artichokes known as tiger nuts.

(El Salvador) this is a rice based sweet beverage (usually served

in a plastic bag). Watch out for the purity of the water.

(Costa Rica) clear alcoholic beverage made from corn.

Be careful, this can be dangerous!

horchata de almendra, beverage made of ground almonds

hormiga culona, *(Columbia)* fried ants! *gracias, pero no.*

hormigas rojas, *(Mexico)* red ants (served live) w/salt & lime

hornazo, cake (served at Easter)

horno, al, baked/roasted

horno, baked/oven

hortaliza, greens

huachinango, *(Mexico)* red snapper.

    a la Veracruzana (Veracruz style) w/tomato sauce,

      capers, green olives, onions & yellow peppers

huerta, w/assorted vegetables

hueso, bone

huevas, fish roe/fish eggs

huevas prensadas, tuna roe/tuna eggs

huevo hilgado, *(Latin America)* garnish of shredded boiled eggs

huevos, eggs

huevos a la española, eggs stuffed w/tomatoes &

    served w/a cheese sauce

huevos a la flamenca, eggs baked w/tomatoes, vegetables & sausage

huevos a la mexicana, *(Mexico)* scrambled eggs w/onions & peppers

huevos al salmorejo, baked eggs w/asparagus, pork sausage & ham

huevos cocidos, hard-boiled eggs

huevos con tocino, eggs & bacon

huevos de mújol, Mediterranean caviar (grey mullet roe)

huevos duros, hard-boiled eggs

huevos duros con mayonesa, hard boiled eggs with mayonnaise

huevos escalfados, poached eggs

huevos estilo extremeña, vegetables w/ham & eggs

huevos fritos, fried eggs

huevos motuleños, *(Mexico) tortilla,* fried eggs,

    black beans, ham & tomato sauce (a breakfast dish)

huevos pasados por agua, soft-boiled eggs

huevos pericos, *(Latin America)* scrambled eggs

huevos poché, poached eggs

huevos por agua, soft-boiled eggs

67

huevos rancheros, *(Mexico)* fried eggs served w/a hot tomato sauce.

"Rancher's eggs", served to laborers in the morning. Today it is
served in the morning & as a snack at any time

huevos rellenos, deviled eggs

huevos revueltos, scrambled eggs

huit la coche, mushroom-like corn fungas

huit la coche is very popular at the moment.

humita, *(Chile)* ground corn wrapped in a corn husk & boiled.

Highly seasoned. *(Ecuador)* sweet corn *tamales*

húngaros, *(Uruguay)* spicy sausage

infusiones, herbal teas

inglesa, a la, rare meat/served w/boiled vegetables

intxaursalsa, *(Basque)* walnut cream

IVA, (VAT) Value Added Tax. *IVA no incluido* means VAT not included

jabalí, boar

jaiba, *(Latin America)* crab

jalapeño, *(Mexico)* green, very hot pepper. Of the over 60 varieties of
chilies found in *Mexico*, this one is hot, but not murderously so

jalea, jelly

jamón, ham (cured)

jamón cocido, boiled ham

jamón de York, cooked ham on the bone

jamón en dulce, ham boiled & served cold

jamón gallego, smoked ham

jamón serrano, thin slices of cured ham (like prosciutto)

japuta (means son of a bitch), pomfret (seafood)

Don't miss the Museo de Jamón in Madrid, an interesting and popular restaurant near the Plaza del Sol.

jarabe, syrup of fresh fruit

jardinera, a la, served w/vegetables

jarra, carafe/pitcher

jarrete, hock/shin bone

jengibre, ginger

jerez, sherry

 *jerez.*

jerez, al, braised in sherry

jerez almontillado, older *jerez fino*.

    Aged at least eight years in wood

    w/a gold color & nutty flavor

jerez fino, pale dry sherry

jerez manzanilla, slightly sharper sherry than *jerez fino*

jerez oloroso, dark, full-bodied sherry.

    Most are sweet. The best are dry

jerez palo cortado, a rare sherry, light & gold w/a complex "character"

jeta, pigs'cheek

jibia, cuttlefish

jícama, *(Mexico)* a root vegetable similar to a potato, usually eaten raw.

    (Latin America) sweet tropical fruit

jitomate, *(Latin America)* tomato

jobo, *(Puerto Rico)* hogplum. A type of plum.

    This fruit is oval, yellow & a couple of

    inches long & is usually used to make jelly

judías, dried beans

judías blancas, white beans

judías negras, black beans

judías rojas, red beans

judías verdes, green or string beans

judiones, broad beans

jueye, *(Puerto Rico)* land crab

jugo, juice/fruit juice/gravy

jugo de fruta, fruit juice

jugo de naranja, orange juice

jugo de tomate, tomato juice

jugo, en su, in its own juice

juliana, w/shredded vegetables

julivert, parsley

jugo de
naranja
yron.

jurel, mackerel

kaki, persimmons

kirsch, cherry liqueur

kokotxas, *Basque* dish of tender glands near
    the throat of cod *No, we're not Kidding.*

kuchen, *(Latin America)* pie

lacón, ham (boiled)/pork shoulder

lacón curado, salted pork

lamprea, lamprey (seafood)

lamprea de mer, eel

langosta, lobster

lamprea.

langosta a Arragón, lobster in a pepper sauce

langosta a la Catalana, lobster in ham, mushroom & white sauce

langosta a la Costa Brava, lobster in tomato sauce

langosta a la vasca, lobster in a seafood sauce

langosta con pollo, lobster & chicken in a tomato stew

langostinos, shrimp/prawns. *(Chile)* baby crayfish

lapa, *(Venezuela)* large roasted rodent! *NO, THANKS.*

lardo, lard

laurel, hojas de, bay leaves

lebrato.

lebrada de progonaos, rabbit stew in wine sauce

lebrato, rabbit

lechal/lechazo, milk-fed lamb

leche, milk

leche desnatada, skim milk

leche enter, whole milk

leche frita, custard w/hard crust & creamy inside

 liebre.

leche merengada/leche meringuada, cold milk w/meringues (ice-milk)

leche quemada, *(Mexico)* dessert made of vanilla & sugar

lechecillas de ternera, calf's sweetbreads

lechón, pork. *(Ecuador)* suckling pig

70

lechón al horno, *(Bolivia)* roast pork w/sweet potatoes

lechón asado, roast suckling pig

lechona, *(Latin America)* suckling pig

lechona asada, roast suckling pig

lechosa, papaya fruit

lechuga, lettuce

legumbres, vegetables

lemón, lemon

lechón.

lengua, tongue. *(Mexico)* usually served in chili sauce

lenguado, sole

lentejas, lentils

lentejas onubenses, lentils w/spicy sausage & onions

levadura, yeast/baking powder/any leavening agent

levadura quimica, baker's yeast

liadillos, stuffed meat/cabbage rolls

liba, sea bass

licor, liquor

licor de petalos, rose petal liquor

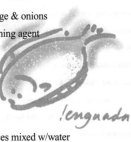

lenguado

licuado, *(Latin America)* milk shake/fruit juices mixed w/water

liebre, rabbit

lima, lime

lima.

limón, lemon

limonada, lemonade

limon.

lisa, grey mullet. *(Venezuela)* tap beer

liscos, omelette w/bacon

lista de platos, menu

lista de precios, list of prices

listo de vinos, wine list

liviano, light beverage

llagosta, lobster dish

llagosta a la catalona, crayfish w/wine & chocolate

llamantol, lobster

llapingacho, *(Ecuador)* mashed potatoes w/cheese (w/a fried egg on top)

llegumet, beans, rice & potato dish

lobarro, bass

locha, loach (carp)/cod

locrio de cerdo, *(Dominican Republic)* pork & rice dish

locro, *(Latin America)* corn & meat soup. *(Paraguay)* corn stew.
    (Ecuador) corn or potato soup w/cheese & avocado

lombarda, red cabbage

lomo, loin. *(Uruguay)* the best cut of meat. *Lomito* is tenderloin

lomo a lo pobre, *(Chile)* beef topped w/two eggs, served w/french fries

lomo bajo, sirloin

lomo curado, cured pork sausage

lomo de cerdo con leche, pork loin pot roast in milk

lomo embuchado, cured smoked pork loin

lomo montado, *(Bolivia)* "mounted steak" tenderloin
    w/two eggs on top &
    served w/rice & fried bananas

lomo saltado, *(Peru)* stir-fried steak served
    w/onions, rice, tomatoes & vegetables

lomo relleno, *(Panama)* steak stuffed
    w/spices & herbs (especially cilantro)

lonch, *(Mexico)* lunch

lonchas de jamón, slices of cured ham

longaniza, long spicy sausage

lonja, thick slice of meat

lubina, sea bass

lubina albufera, sea bass w/paprika sauce

lubina a la cantábrica, bass w/white wine, lemon & garlic

lubina a la marinera, bass in a parsley sauce

lucia/lucio, pike

The food on the western coast of South America has been heavily influenced by immigrants from the orient.

macarones/macarrones, macaroni

macarrones gratinados, macaroni & cheese

macedonia de frutas, fruit salad

machacón, boiled potato dish

machas, *(Chile)* clams

machas.

macho, *(Latin America)* large green bananas

madrileña, a la, w/tomatoes, sausage & paprika/w/peppers

madrileño, w/lemon & oil

maduro, ripe

magdalenas, sponge cakes/muffins

magras con tomate, fried ham in a tomato sauce

maíz.

magro, lean

magro con tomate, fried ham in tomato

mahón, mild cheese

mahonesa, mayonesa, mayonnaise

maíz, corn

maíz is arguably the most important food export of the western hemisphere.

majarete, *(Dominican Republic)* cornmeal, custard dessert

málaga, sweet dessert wine

mallorquina, a la, highly seasoned seafood

malta, *(Puerto Rico)* malt beverage w/malt, barley, sugar cane
& hops (non-alcoholic). In *Latin America*, dark beer

malteada, *(Latin America)* milk shake

malvasia, sweet dessert wine

mamey, *(Ecuador, Puerto Rico)* sweet red/orange
tropical fruit (mammee apple)

mamey

mandarina, tangerine

mandioca, *(Paraguay)* cassava, a starchy, boiled root
served like mashed potatoes

mango, mango. In South *Puerto Rico*, the mangos have a flavor
similar to pineapples

maní (manises), peanut (peanuts)

73

manitas de cerdo, pig's feet

manitas de cordero, leg of lamb

manjar blanco, *(Columbia)* a soft toffee dessert.

(Peru) sweet dessert made from condensed milk

manojo, bunch/handful

manos de cerdo, pig's feet

manteca, *(Argentina, Uruguay)* butter

mantecado, vanilla ice cream/small butter cakes/creamy
cinnamon-flavored custard

mantequilla, butter

manzana en dulce, apple in honey

manzanas, apples

manzanas asadas, baked apples

manzanilla, herbal tea (camomile tea)

manzanilla, pale dry sherry (slightly sharper sherry than *jerez fino*)

manzanillas, green olives known as the Seville olive

maracuya, *(Latin America)* passion fruit

margarina, margarine

margarita, tequila w/lime juice

maria, whiting

mar i muntanya, *(Catalan)* dish of shrimp & chicken

marinera, a la, This can mean many different
things. Usually it means w/tomatoes,
herbs, onions & wine. Can also mean
cooked w/seafood in hot sauce

mariscada, mixed shellfish/shellfish in a parsley, wine, olive oil
& garlic sauce. *(El Salvador)* seafood soup

mariscos, seafood. *Mariscos del día* means fresh seafood

mar i terra, chicken & seafood dish

marmitako, *Basque* tuna casserole

marquesa de chocolate, chocolate mousse

mantequilla.

margarita.
Que bueno!

a la marinera
means
Sailor style.

74

marrajo, shark

marrón, *(Venezuela)* a large cup of strong coffee w/a small amount of milk

marroncito, *(Venezuela)* small cup of strong coffee w/a small amount of milk

maruca, large cod

más, more

masa, pastry/dough/pasta. *(Mexico)* corn dough used to make *tortillas*

matalahuga, matalahuva, anise

matambre, beef roll stuffed w/vegetables

maté, *(Latin America)* caffeinated drink similar to tea &
   made from the leaves of a member of the holly
   family. *(Paraguay)* *maté* is served in a gourd

maté.
is very
bitter.

maté de coca, *(Latin America)* coca leaf tea

mat mulo, very fresh

mavi, *(Puerto Rico)* beer made from tree bark

mayonesa, mayonnaise

mazamorra, *(Columbia)* thick meat & corn soup

mazamorra morada, *(Peru)* fruit pudding made from purple corn

mazapán, marzipan

mechada, although this can mean any number of things, it most often
   refers to a roast

medallones, medallions/small steaks/fish steaks

media, half

media botella, half-bottle

medialuna, *(Argentina)* breakfast croissant

media luna
means half
moon.

media noche, *(Puerto Rico)* pork, ham & cheese sandwich

mejillones, mussels

mejorana, marjoram

melaza, molasses

mel i mató, cream cheese w/honey

melindres, marzipan biscuits

melocotón, peach

marjoram is
closely related
to oregano.

75

melón, melon

melón al calisay, melon w/liquor poured on top

membrillo, quince

menestra, vegetable soup

menestra, as in minestrone. (handwritten note)

menestra de Tudela, asparagus stew

menjar blanco, dessert w/cream, lemons & ground almonds

menta, mint.

Menta poleo is mint tea

menú, menu

menú de la casa, often means fixed price menu

menú del día, menu of the day

menú fijo, fixed price menu

menú turístico, tourist menu (usually fixed price)

menudillos, chicken giblets

menudo, offal/tripe (the lining of an animal's stomach). *(Mexico)* tripe soup

Some people consider menudo to be a cure for hangovers. (handwritten note)

menudos gitanos, tripe w/ham, garlic, saffron & cumin

merengada, *(Latin America)* fruit juice, milk & sugar

merengues, meringues

merienda, snack. *(Mexico)* usually a late evening snack

merlano, whiting (seafood)

merluza, cod or whiting

merluza a la castellana, cod w/shrimp, clams, eggs & chili

merluza a la gallega, cod w/potatoes & paprika

merluza a la vasca, cod in a white wine & parsley sauce

merluza a la koskera, *Basque* dish of cod w/cla

merluza en salsa verde, cod in a parsley sauce

mermelada, marmalade/jam

mero, grouper/perch/sea bass

mero. (handwritten note)

mero a la levantina, grouper w/rosemary & lemon juice

mesa, table

mescal/mezcal, *(Mexico)* alcoholic beverage made from
the agave (maguey) plant (similar to grappa)

mezclado, mixed

michelada, *(Mexico)* beer, ice & lime juice

michirones, beans stewed w/chili peppers & sausage

miel, honey

mielga, a type of shark

miera cielo, cod & red pepper salad

migas, croûtons/sautéed breadcrumbs

migas canas, bread pudding w/milk & breadcrumbs

mijo, millet

milanesa, *(Argentina, Paraguay, Uruguay)* breaded & fried veal cutlet

milanesa, a la, can mean either breaded & fried or served w/cheese

milanesa de carne, *(Argentina)* sliced beef, breaded & then deep fried

milanesa de pollo, *(Argentina)* slices of chicken, breaded & then deep fried

milanesa res, *(Mexico)* breaded and fried steak

minuta, menu

minutas, *(El Salvador)* honey flavored drink made w/crushed ice

mistela, wine & grape juice

mixiotes, *(Mexico)* pieces of chicken served in a spicy sauce

mixto, mixed (can also mean a combination of meats)

mofongo, *(Dominican Republic, Puerto Rico)* mashed &
then roasted plantain
w/spices & *chicharrones*

mogollas, *(Columbia)* wheat rolls w/raisins

mojama, blue fin tuna

mojara a la plancha, *(Mexico)* grilled ocean perch

mojarra, bream/fresh water fish/ bluegills

mojete, cod, peppers & onion salad/vegetable dip

mojo, a sauce w/its main ingredient of spicy peppers

mojo colorado, mixture of paprika, cumin & chilli peppers

mielga.

*generally,
anything "a la
plancha"
is
grilled.*

mojo isleño, *(Puerto Rico)* sauce of onions, olives, capers, tomatoes, garlic & vinegar

muy sabroso!

mojojones, mussels

mole, thick, dark complex chili sauces invented in *Mexico*

mole poblano, chicken w/sauce of chili pepper, chocolate & spices. Turkey is substituted for chicken in ***mole poblano de guajolote***

mole verde, *(Mexico)* green sauce w/many ingredients including *tomatillos*

moll, red mullet

mollejas, sweetbreads. *(Latin America)* blood sausage

molusco, snail, mussel or clam (mollusk)

mondongo, *(Dominican Republic, Puerto Rico, Latin America)* seasoned tripe stew

mongetes/monjetes, dried white beans

montilla, dessert wine

mora, blackberry

moraga de sardines, sardine casserole

morcilla, blood sausage/black pudding (made from blood, onions & rice)

morcilla de ternera, blood sausage made from calves' blood

morcilla dulce, *(Uruguay)* sweet blood sausage

morcón, a spiced ham

morena, moray eel

morena.

moreno, almond meringue

morilla, morel mushroom

moro, "Moors". In *Spain*, you will find reference to *moro* or the Moors who dominated *Spain* for over 700 years. This term can mean many things, but frequently means a spicy sauce

moros y cristianos, black beans & white rice

morragote.

morragote, grey mullet

morro, cheek

mortadela, salami

morteruelo, mixed meat hash

moscatel, sweet dessert wine

mosh, *(Guatemala)* oats w/honey & cinnamon

mostachones, "S" shaped biscuits

mostaza, mustard

mosto, grape juice

muchacho, *(Venezuela)* beef loin roasted & served in a sauce

mújol, grey mullet

musclos, chicken legs. *(Catalon)* mussels

muslo, drumstick of poultry

musola, a type of shark

muy hecho, meat well done

muy seco, very dry

muzzarella, *(Latin America)* mozzarella

nabo, turnip

nacatamales, *(Latin America) tortilla* filled w/meat,

　　corn & sauce & steamed

　　in banana leaves or a corn husk

nachos, *(Mexico) tortilla* chips w/*frijoles refritos,*

　　grated cheese, *jalapeños, guacamole,*

　　black olives & sour cream

ñame, *(Dominican Republic)* yam

naranja, orange.

　　Naranja agria (sour orange) is a common

　　seasoning used in *Mexico & Puerto Rico*

naranjada, orangeade

naranjilla, *(Ecuador)* citrus fruit juice (a cross between peach & orange)

nata, cream

nata batida, whipped cream

natillas, pudding/spiced custard

natural, raw or fresh

navajas, razor clams

navarra, a la, stuffed w/ham

[handwritten notes:] Mosh may sound exotic but in English it's mosh. and that spells Oatmeal in our book.

muslo.

Naranja.

79

nécoras, spider crabs/sea crabs

nectarinas, nectarines

negrito, *(Venezuela)* small cup of strong black coffee

nieves, *(Mexico)* sorbet (means "snow")

níscalo, wild mushroom

níspero, *(Puerto Rico)* sapodilla (a rough-skinned,
    brown fruit from a tropical evergreen tree)

nixtamal, *(Latin America)* corn meal dough

nopales, *(Mexico)* sliced & cooked cactus leaves

nopalito, cactus leaf salad

ñoquis, *(Argentina)* the same as the Italian gnocchi (potato dumplings)

ñora, mild & sweet peppers

nueces, walnuts

nuez, nut

nuez moscada, nutmeg

oca, goose

ocopa, *(Peru)* potatoes or eggs in a spicy sauce

oliaigua, water-based soup flavored w/garlic,
    parsley & olive oil. A specialty
    in the *Balearic Islands*

olímpicos, *(Uruguay)* club sandwiches

olivas, olives

olla, stew. Named after the clay pot

olla de carne, *(Costa Rica)* beef stew usually w/plantains & yucca

olla de trigo, chickpea soup w/sausage & bacon

olla gitana, thick vegetable stew

olla podrida (putrid pot), stew of meat, poultry, ham & vegetables

olleta, thick, chunky vegetable soup

oloroso, full-bodied sherry. Some are sweet. The best are dry

omelette, *(Latin America)* omelette.

    Remember, omelette in *Spain* is a *tortilla*

once, las, *(Chile)* Once means eleven – *aguardiente* has eleven letters. So, when someone says that he is having his "*once*", it means that he is having a drink of *aguardiente*. *Once* also refers to snacks served in the late afternoon or early evening. Tea or coffee is served with cookies, toast, cheese or other small appetizers

oporto, port

orégano, oregano

If you encounter the letter "O" on a menu it probably means "OR".

orejas (de cerdo), pigs' ear

orejones, dried apricots

ortelletes, deep fried pastry flavored with anise

ortiga, nettle

orujo, potent alcoholic beverage made from grapes

oscuro, dark (in color)

OSTIONES.

ostiones, *(Dom. Republic, Puerto Rico),* small local oysters.

   (South America) scallops

ostras, oysters

ous, *(Catalan)* egg

pa amb tomàquet is Catalan for Bread & Tomatoes.

oveja, ewe

pa amb tomàquet, toast snack w/tomato sauce, olive oil, ham & cheese

pabellón/pabellón criolla, *(Columbia, Venezuela)* shredded beef in a spicy tomato sauce w/rice, plantains & beans

pacanas, pecans

pachamanca, *(Peru)* stew of meat and vegetables cooked in clay pots

pacharán, alcoholic beverage made from the blackthorn fruit (sloeberries)

pacumutu, *(Latin America)* beef on a skewer

pa d'ous, flan

paella, saffron flavored rice w/assorted seafood (or w/meat).

   This Spanish specialty is named

   after the *paellera,* the pan in

   which *paella* is made

paella.

paella a la catalana, *paella* w/tomatoes, pork, sausage, squid, red peppers

81

paella a la Valenciana, *paella* w/fish & meat
(usually assorted shellfish & chicken)

SiN Trabajo means without work.

paella al estilo de Parellada/paella sin trabajo,
paella w/out shells or bones

paella alicantina, *paella* w/fish, onions, green peppers & tomatoes

paella castelana, *paella* w/meat

paella marinera, *paella* w/fish

pagre, bream

paico, *(Ecuador)* lemon & anise flavored *aguardiente*

paila, *(Latin America)* fried eggs w/bread

pajaritos, small birds

pajuil, *(Puerto Rico)* cashew

palacones de plátano, *(Panama)* fried plantain

palaia petit, sole

paleta/paletillo, shoulder or breast

palitos, skewer

palmeras de hojaldre, puff pastry dessert

palmitos, hearts of palm

palo cortado, sweet, rare sherry, light & gold w/a complex "character"

paloma, pigeon

palometa, deep-water fish

palometa blanca

palometa blanca, pompano

palometa negra, pomfret, a black spiny fish

palomitas, popcorn

palomitas means little doves.

palta, avocado

palta a la jardinera, *(Peru)* avocado stuffed w/vegetable salad

palta a rellena, *(Peru)* avocado stuffed w/chicken salad

pan, bread. ***Barra de pan*** is a loaf of bread

pana, *(Chile)* liver

panaché de verduras, vegetable stew/mixed vegetables

pana de coco, *(Nicaragua)* coconut bread

82

pan a la Francesa, *(Mexico)* french toast

pan aléman, dark bread

panapen, *(Puerto Rico)* breadfruit

pan blanco, white bread

panceta, bacon/pork belly

pancita, *(Latin America)* tripe

pancitos, rolls

} you don't want to mix these two up!

pan de agua, *(Puerto Rico)* french bread

pan de azúcar, *(Puerto Rico)* sugar dessert bread

pan de coco, *(Central America)* coconut bread

pan de centeno, rye bread

pan de higos, dried fig cake

pan de horno, *(Chile)* baked bread

barra de pan.

pan de leche, *(Argentina)* a cream topped muffin eaten at breakfast

pan de pernil, jellied ham

pan dulce, sweet bread

panecicos, fried sweet puff dessert

panecillos, rolls/small loaf of bread

pan integral, whole wheat bread

pan negro, dark bread

pan rallado, bread crumbs

panquemado, sugar glazed bread

panqueques, *(South America)* pancakes

panqueques. Such a cute word, too!

panucho, *(Mexico)* deep fried *tortilla* filled w/refried beans, meat, tomatoes, sour cream & onions

papa, *(Latin America)* potato

papas a la criolla, *(Latin America)* potatoes in a spicy sauce

papas a la huancaína, *(Peru)* spicy potato dish w/cheese and chili sauce

papas arrugadas, spicy potato dish

papas bravas, *(Latin America)* potatoes in cayenne pepper

papas fritas, french fries/potato chips

papas rellenas, *(Peru)* stuffed potatoes

papaya, papaya fruit

papazul, *(Mexico)* tortilla filled w/diced hard-boiled eggs & covered w/a
mild chili sauce popular in the Yucatán peninsula

parcha, *(Puerto Rico)* passion fruit

pardet, grey mullet

pargo, sea bream/red snapper

pardet.

parilla, a la, grilled

parilla criolla, *(Venezuela)* marinated beef cooked on a grill

parillada, *(Latin America)* mixed charcoal grill of meats, including steak. A
word of advice, in some Latin American countries, this often contains organ meats not often eaten in the United States & Canada.
In Spain this can refer to a grilled selection of fish

parillada mixta, mixed grill

parrochas, small sardines

pasa de corinto, currant

pasado, done, cooked

pasado bien, well done

pasado poco, rare

pasas, dried fruit/raisins

pasta, pasta/soup noodles/can also mean pastry

pasta quebrada, a flaky pastry

pastel, pie/cake

parrochas.

pastel.

pastel de choclo, *(Chile)* a corn casserole filled w/meats & vegetables

pastel de higado, liver pâté

pastel de pasas, raisin pudding

pastelería, pastry

pasteles, pastries. *(Puerto Rico)* tamales made from plantains

pastelillos, small tarts. *(Puerto Rico)* deep fried turnovers containing meat,
fish &/or cheese (and often fruit & jam)

pastelito, cookies/cupcakes

pastel murciano, pastry pie filled w/sausage, onions & meat

pastelón de vegetables, *(Dominican Republic)* vegetable pastry

pastel vasco, filled sweet pastry

pasticho, *(Venezuela)* a dish which is very similar to lasagna

pastilla, bar (as in candy bar) or small candy

pastor, al, usually means a pork-based dish

pata, foot

patacó, tuna casserole

patacones, *(Ecuador)* fried plantains w/cheese.
   (Columbia) mashed potatoes & plantains

patacu, tuna casserole

patas de cordero, stewed leg of lamb

patatas, potatoes

patatas a la leonesa, potatoes w/onions

patatas a la pescadora, potatoes w/fish

patatas a la riojana, potato & sausage dish

patatas alli olli, potatoes in mayonnaise

patatas bravas, spicy potatoes w/paprika

patatas castellanas, potatoes & paprika

patatas fritas, french fries

patatas nuevas, new potatoes

patatas pobres, potatoes w/garlic & parsley

patatas puré, mashed potatoes

patatas viudas, potatoes w/fried onions

patín, *(Latin America)* tomato-based sauce

patitos rellenos, stuffed duckling

pato, duck

pato a la naranja/pato a la servillana, duck à l'orange

pavías de pescado, fried fish sticks

pavipollo, large chicken

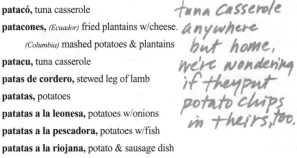

We've never had tuna casserole anywhere but home, we're wondering if they put potato chips in theirs, too.

pato.

pavo, turkey

pavo relleno a la catalana, turkey w/sausage, plum & pork stuffing

pavo trufado, turkey w/truffle stuffing

pay, *(Mexico)* pie

pazole, *(Mexico)* chicken or pork stew w/chopped vegetables & herbs

pebre, oil & paprika sauce

pecho, breast/brisket

pecho de cerdo, pork belly

pecho de ternera, veal breast

pechuga, breast

pechuga de pollo, chicken breast

peix rei, whiting

peixina de pelegri, scallops

pellofa, *Balearic Island* drink of gin w/ice, sugar & lemon

pelotas, meatballs

pepián, *(Latin America)* meat stew

pepinillo, pickle

pepino, cucumber. *(Ecuador)* sweet striped cucumber-like jungle fruit

pepitas, sunflower seeds/pumpkin seeds

pepitoria, stuffed w/tomatoes, green peppers & onions/ fricassee.
This term has many meanings. For instance, *pepitoria de pollo*
is chicken w/almonds

pequeño, small

pera, pear. *Peras al vino* are pears in a sweet wine sauce

perca, perch

percebes, shellfish/barnacle

perdices (perdíu), partridges (partridge)

perdices a la campesina, partridge w/vegetables

perdices a la capellán, ham & pork sausage in a beef roll

perdices a la manchega, partridge cooked in red wine, peppers & herbs

perdices a la Torero, partridge w/tomato, ham & anchovies

España
Balearic islands
mediterranean sea.

peras.

perdigones, partridge

perdiz, partridge

perejil, parsley

perifollo, chervil (an herb)

perilla, a type of bland cheese

pernil, ham/pork shoulder

perrito caliente, hot dog

perruñas/perruñillas, cinnamon cookies

pescadilla, whiting

pescadito, fried fish

pescado, fish

pestiños, sweet anise flavored pastries

petit pois, *(Latin America)* peas

peto, *(Columbia)* white corn soup w/milk

pez, fish

pez angel, angelfish shark

pez espada, swordfish

pez limón, amberjack

pez martillo, hammerhead shark

pez plata, argentine (a fish similar to salmon)

píbil, *(Latin America)* dark sauce

picada, thick sauce of garlic & bread

picadillo, ground meat. *(Latin America)* snacks. *(Costa Rica)* fried vegetables.
  (Mexico) a spicy seasoned ground meat dish (served as either a main
  course or as filling)

picado, ground up

picante, spicy/hot

picante de pollo, *(Bolivia, Peru)* fried chicken served w/fried potatoes & rice.
  Very spicy! *Picantes* can also refer to chicken or shrimp served in a
  spicy red sauce

picarones/picarrones, *(Peru)* deep fried sweet-potato batter served w/syrup

perdigones.

pescado.

*petit pois is
actually
french.*

*Picadillo is one of
our favorite Foods!*

87

picatostes, fried, sugared & buttered toast

pichón, pigeon

pichón con pasas y piñones, pigeon w/raisins & pine nuts

pichoncillo, young pigeon, squab

pichuncho, *(Chile)* pisco & vermouth

pico de gallo, *(Mexico)* tomato, onion, cilantro & scallion relish (*salsa*)

picoso, *(Latin America)* hot, spicy

pie (pies), foot (feet). *(Latin America)* pie

pierna, leg (of beef)

pijama, caramel custard w/ice cream topped w/whipped cream

pijotas, baby cod

pijotas, small whiting

pil-pil, al, prepared w/oil & garlic

pil-pilando, any dish served sizzling hot

piloncillo, *(Latin America)* raw sugar

pilongas, dried chestnuts

pilotas, meatballs

pimentón, paprika/cayenne pepper

pimienta de cayena, cayenne pepper

pimienta inglesa/pimienta jamaica, allspice

pimienta/pimienta negra, black pepper

pimiento, bell pepper

pimiento.

pimiento morrón, sweet red bell pepper

pimientos de piquillo rellenos, fried red peppers stuffed (often w/cod)

pimientos fritos, deep fried green peppers

pimientos rellenos, stuffed peppers

Piña

pimientos rojos asados, roasted red pepper salad

pimientos verde, green peppers

piña, pineapple

piña colada, rum mixed w/pineapple juice & cream of coconut

pinchitos, snacks, appetizers/kebabs

pincho moruno, meat kebab. *Pincho de lomito* is tenderloin shish kebab

pinchos, snacks served on a toothpick/a dish similar to shish kebab, almost
always served w/meat. This is a specialty in *Honduras*.

This is the *Basque* word for *tapas*

pinocillo, *(Latin America)* alcoholic beverage made from toasted seeds

piñon/piñonos, *(Puerto Rico)* plantains layered b/w seasoned ground beef
& rice (deep fried)

pintarroja.

piñonata, pine nut cake

piñones, pine nuts

pintada, guinea hen

pintarroja, small shark

piparrada vasca, tomato & pepper stew w/ham

pipas, seeds

piperita, peppermint

pipián, *(Latin America)* hot chili sauce.

(Dominican Republic) stew containing the intestine of a goat

pipirrana, salad of hard boiled eggs, tomatoes, peppers, onions, tuna,
ham, olive oil & garlic

pique a lo macho, *(Bolivia)* chopped beef served w/onions & vegetables

piquete, *(Columbia)* meat, vegetables & potatoes in a hot pepper sauce

piragua, *(Puerto Rico)* "snow cone" of ice topped w/guava or tamarind syrup

piriñaca, chopped vegetable salad which often contains tuna

pisco, *(Latin America)* colorless & potent alcoholic beverage made from corn
or grapes (often mixed w/orange juice). *(Ecuador)* it is similar to white
rum. *Piscola* is *pisco* and coca-cola

pisco sour, *(Latin America)* lemon juice, sugar & *pisco* shaken together over
ice & topped w/beaten egg whites. A specialty in *Ecuador*

piso, fried vegetables

pistiñes, sweet anise flavored fritters

pisto, mixed vegetable, tomato & eggplant salad

pisto manchego, ratatouille/zucchini, tomato & onion stew

pixin, monkfish

plancha (a la plancha)/planchada, grilled

plátanos, plantains. This vegetable looks like a banana, but it is picked
   when green. Unlike a banana, it is never eaten raw

plátanos flameados, bananas flambéed

plátanos fritos, fried plantains

plátanos horneados, *(Dominican Republic)* baked plantains

platija, flounder

plato, dish/plate

plato montañero, *(Columbia)* a dish w/ground beef,
   sausage, salt pork, beans, rice, avocado & fried
   egg. This dish is also called **bandeja paisa**

plato típico, any dish which is "typical" to the region or country. *(Nicaragua)*
   large & inexpensive meal containing any of the following: beans,
   rice, meat, fried bananas, *tortillas*, cheese & a salad

platos combinados, combination plates

plegonero, cod/whiting

poblano, *(Mexico)* green pepper. Not as hot as a *jalapeño*

pochas, beans

pocillo, *(Puerto Rico)* strong black coffee served after dinner

poco hecho, rare

poco cocido, rare

poco pasado, rare

poleo, mint

poleomenta, mint tea

pollito, young chicken

pollo, chicken

pollo a la mexicana, *(Mexico)* Mexican style chicken cooked w/onions,
   green chili peppers, tomatoes & usually served w/rice & beans

pollo al canario, lemon and chicken. A popular dish in the *Canary Islands*

pollo al chilindrón, cooked chicken w/onions, tomatoes & peppers

Platanado is slang for lazy.

pollo.

90

pollo asado, roast chicken *—borracho means drunk.*

pollo borracho, *(Mexico)* fried chicken in a tequila-based sauce

pollo campurriano, rice w/bacon, chicken, shallots & peppers

pollo en arroz, chicken & rice

pollo en cacerola, chicken casserole

pollo en chanfaina, cooked chicken w/onions, tomatoes & peppers

pollo en pepitoria, chicken in a wine, garlic & saffron sauce

pollo pibil, chicken simmered in spices.

  (Mexico) marinated chicken grilled in banana leaves

pollo reina clamart, roasted chicken w/vegetables

polvorones, hazelnut &/or almond cookies

pomelo, grapefruit

ponche, punch (usually w/brandy)

ponche crema, *(Venezuela)* egg nog

pop, octopus

por favor, please

porcíon, small helping/portion

porotos, *(Latin America)* kidney beans

porra antequerana, *gazpacho* w/raw ham or tomatoes

porrosaldo/porrusaldo, *(Basque)* potato & leek soup (& sometimes cod)

postres, desserts

potaje, vegetable soup/thick soup (like chowder)

pote asturiana, bean & sausage soup

pote con coles, thick cabbage soup

poti poti, salt cod salad w/peppers & potatoes

pozole, *(Latin America)* corn & meat stew/hominy

preserva, preserve

primer plato, starter

pringadas, fried bread w/garlic. After the bread is fried in olive oil

  & garlic, sausage & ham are served on top. Fattening & delicious!

propina, tip. *No incluyen* (or *incluido*) *propina* means tip not included

pop.

We don't know how poti poti tastes but we like the name.

provoleta, *(Latin America)* provolone cheese

pucherete al estilo montañes, spicy blood sausage stew

puchero, stew. *(Uruguay)* beef w/beans, vegetables, sausage & bacon

puchero bogotana, *(Columbia)* boiled vegetables, meat & potatoes

puchero canario, meat & chickpea casserole. A *Canary Islands* specialty

pudín, pudding. **Pudín de arroz,** rice pudding

puerco, pork

puerco chuk, *(Latin America)* pork stew

puerro, leek

pulpeta, slice of meat

pulpito, baby octopus

pulpo, octopus

pulpo de feira, octopus w/paprika & olive oil

pulque, *(Mexico)* alcoholic beverage distilled from the pulp of the
    agave (maguey) plant. It is much thicker than tequila, which is
    also from the agave plant

punta de diamante, diamond shaped meringue cake

punta de espárrago, asparagus tip

puntas de filete de res, *(Mexico)* beefsteak (usually sirloin tips)
    w/guacamole & beans

puntillitas, small squid

punto de nieve, whipped cream w/beaten egg whites

pupusa, *(Central America)* fried *tortillas* filled w/cheese, beans and/or meat.
    You will find *pupusas* & *pupuserías* (snack stands selling *pupusas*)
    everywhere in *El Salvador*. *(Honduras)* *pupusas* are almost always
    filled w/pork

puré de patatas/puré de papas, mashed potatoes

purée de apio, *(Venezuela)* celery root which is boiled, puréed & served
    w/salt & butter. Some think this tastes like chestnuts

puro de caña, *(Latin America),* alcoholic beverage made from sugar cane

purrusalda, *(Basque)* cod, potato & leek soup

queimada, brandy, sugar & lemon drink

quemada, topped w/caramelized cream

queque, *(Latin America)* cake

quesada, cheesecake (a dessert made w/cheese, honey & butter)

quesadilla, *(Mexico)* grilled or fried *tortilla* filled w/meat, cheese, potatoes and/or chilies. *(Spain)* cheesecake

quesillo, *(Venezuela)* steamed *flan*. This can also refer to cheese

quesillo de leche y piña, *(Dominican Republic)* milk & pineapple flan

queso, cheese

queso blanco, white cheese

queso de burgos, soft, white, creamy cheese

queso de cabrales, blue cheese (not as strong as Roquefort)

queso de camerano, goat cheese

queso de Cantabria, mild cheese made from cows' cream

queso de cervera, soft ewes' milk cheese

queso de hoja, *(Puerto Rico)* mild soft cheese

queso de Idiazábal, strong, creamy, smoky cheese

queso de mahón, semi-hard, tangy cheese

queso de mató, goat milk cheese

queso de oveja, mild sheep cheese

queso de pasiego, fresh, soft cheese

queso de pichón, creamy, blue cheese.

queso de puzol, fresh cows' milk cheese

queso de Roncal, strong, creamy sheeps' cheese (low-fat)

queso de San Simón, strong, smoky cheese

queso de tetilla, white cows' milk cheese

queso de Tresviso-Pícon, a blue cheese

queso de villalón, soft cheese made from sheep's milk

queso del país, local cheese

queso fresco, *(Mexico)* white cheese (similar to feta cheese)

queso fundido, *(Mexico)* baked cheese dip

queso.

queso gallego, a creamy cheese

queso Ibores, goat's milk cheese w/a paprika coated rind

queso manchego, hard, salty, rich & nutty flavor. *Spain's best known*

quilet, bream

quisquilla, shrimp

raba, breaded, fried squid

rábano, radish. *Rabanitos* are small radishes found in *Latin America*

rábano picante, horse radish

rabo, tail

rabo de buey/rabo de toro, oxtail

racimo, bunch (as in a bunch of grapes)

raciónes, large portion (usually of snacks)

*racion piqueña
on a menu
means small
portion.*

ragout, ragoût

raíz, root

rajas, slices. In some parts of *Latin America*,
    grilled green peppers

rallado, grated

rama, dried hot chili peppers

ramillo, spicy

rana, ancas de, frog legs

rancho canario, stew of sausage, bacon,
    beans, potatoes & pasta.
    A specialty in the *Canary Islands*

rap/rape, monkfish/anglefish

raspas de anchoas, deep fried backbones of anchovies

ravioles, ravioli

raya, ray, skate (seafood)

rebanada, slice   *raya.*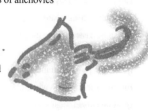

rebozado, coated w/breadcrumbs & fried

recargo, extra charge

redondo, filet of beef

refrescos, soft drink/cool drink. *(Costa Rica)* fruit shakes. *(Puerto Rico)* you will find *refrescos del país* signs everywhere. These drink stands are often automobile trunks filled w/various fruit juices, especially *cocos fríos* (cold drinking coconuts)

refritos, *(Latin America)* refried beans

regular, meat done medium

rehogado, sautéed

rellenas/os, stuffed/filled

rellenos de papa, *(Puerto Rico)* meat stuffed potatoes fried in batter

rémol, brill/flounder

remolachas, beets

reo, sea trout

repollo, cabbage

remolachas

repostería de la casa, house specialty desserts

requemado, cold rice pudding w/sugar topping

requesónes, cottage cheese

res, beef

reserva, mature wine (of older vintage)

revoltillo, scrambled eggs

revueltos, scrambled eggs

revuelto mixto, scrambled eggs w/vegetables

riñón, kidney

riñonada, roasted kidneys

rioja, a red wine similar to Bordeaux

rioja, a la (a la riojana), served w/red peppers

róbalo, haddock/snook

robioles, custard filled pastry

rocoto, *(Latin America)* a hot red pepper

Róbalo

rodaballo, turbot/flounder

rollitos, small filled rolls

rollo de carne, meat loaf

romana, a la, dipped in batter & then fried

romero, rosemary

romesco, mild, sweet chili pepper. This can also refer to a sauce of peppers, tomatoes, ground almonds & hazelnuts

romesco de pescado, mixed fish. *Romesco de peix* is a fish stew popular in the *Catalonia* region of *Spain*

ron, rum

ropa vieja, left-over meat & vegetables cooked w/tomatoes & green peppers. *(Panama)* rice covered w/spicy shredded beef & green peppers

ropa vieja means old clothes.

rosada, shark

rosado, rosé wine

rosbif, roast beef

rosca/rosco, doughnut

roscon, *(Columbia)* roll filled w/guava jelly & coated w/sugar

rosé, rosé wine

rosquilla, doughnut (usually glazed)

rossejat, cooked rice dish

rovellon, wild mushroom

rubio, red mullet

ruibarbo, rhubarb

sábalo, shad (seafood)

Sabores or Sabroso means savory or tasty.

sacarina, saccharin

saice, *(Bolivia)* a spicy meat broth

sajta, *(Bolivia)* chicken served in *aji* (hot pepper) sauce

sal, salt

saladitos, appetizers

salado, salted

salazón, cured (salted fish or meat)

salchicha, pork sausage

salchichas blancas, pork sausage w/fried onions

salchichas de Frankfurt, hot dogs, frankfurters

salchichón, salami (cured sausage)

salema, bream

salmón, salmon

Salmón.

salmón ahumado, smoked salmon

salmón a la ribereña, fried salmon steaks

salmonete, red mullet/goalfish

salmonete en papillote, red mullet cooked in foil

salmorejo, thick sauce of bread, tomatoes, vinegar, green peppers, olive oil & garlic

salmorejo cordobes, chilled *gazpacho*

salmorreta, a smoky tomato sauce

Salpicon means a scattering.

salmuera, in brine

salones, cured lamb or beef

salpicón de mariscos, mixed shellfish salad

salsa, sauce. *(Mexico)* relish of chopped tomatoes, onions, cilantro & scallions & also called *pico de gallo, salsa crud,* or *salsa fresca*

salsa bechamel, white sauce/béchamel sauce

salsa criolla, *(Uruguay)* spicy sauce used on steaks

salsa de tomate, ketchup/tomato sauce

salsa española, sauce w/wine, spices & herbs

salsa hollandaise, hollandaise sauce

salsa ingles, *(Mexico)* Worcestershire sauce

salsa mayordoma, butter & parsley sauce

salsa picante, hot pepper sauce

salsa ranchero, *(Mexico)* red chili sauce w/a tomato base

salsa romesco, sauce w/tomatoes & garlic or ground nuts & sweet peppers

salsa tártara, tartar sauce

salsa verde, parsley sauce. *(Mexico)* chilies, cilantro, garlic & green tomato sauce. *(Latin America)* hot sauce w/tomatoes & peppers

salsifí, salsify

salteado/a, sautéed

salteño, *(Latin America)* turnover filled w/meat & sauce

salvado, bran

salvia, sage

sama de pluma, bream

samfaina, sauce of eggplant, zucchini, peppers, onions, tomatoes

sancochado, *(Peru)* meat & vegetable stew w/spices

sancocho, *(Latin America)* vegetable soup w/meat or fish. *(Puerto Rico)* beef soup. *(Canary Islands)* white fish & boiled potatoes

sancocho canario, fish stew w/potatoes in a red pepper sauce

sandía, watermelon

sandwich, sandwich

sandwich caliente, hot sandwich. *(Uruguay)* grilled ham & cheese sandwich

sandwich mixto, often refers to a ham & cheese sandwich

sange, blood

sangría, chilled red wine, fruit juice, brandy & soda. There are many variations. For example, in *Ecuador*, red wine, sugar, fruit & lemon juice

sangrita, tequila w/lime, orange & tomato juice

santiaguiño, (clawless) lobster

sard, bream

sardinas, sardines

sargo, bream

sarsuela, fish stew (see also *zarzuela*)

sarten, en, from the frying pan

schop, *(Chile)* beer (usually draft beer)

sebo, fat

seco, dry. Can also refer to dry wine

seco de, stew

seco de cordero, *(Ecuador)* lamb stew

seco de gallina, *(Ecuador)* chicken stew

semi-dulce, semi-sweet

98

semillas, seeds

sémola/semolina, ground duram wheat

sencillo, plain

sepia, cuttlefish

sequillos, hazelnut meringues

serenata, *(Puerto Rico)* fish in vinaigrette w/onions, avocados & vegetables

serrano, thin slices of cured ham (like prosciutto). *(Mexico)* a small, green chili pepper which is hotter than a *jalapeño*

servicio, service

servicio incluido, service included (tip included)

servicio no incluido, service not included (tip not included)

servilleta, napkin

sesamo, sesami. Can also refer to perch

sesos, brains *No me gusta!*

setas, mushrooms

setas a la bordalesa, mushrooms cooked in red wine & onions

setas salteadas, mushrooms w/sausage & garlic

seviche, *(Mexico)* cold white fish salad popular in Acapulco. *See* **ceviche**

sevillana, a la, cooked in wine w/olives

sidra, cider

sifón, soda water

silpancho, *(Bolivia)* beef (thinly sliced & breaded) served w/an egg on top

sincronizadas, *(Mexico)* flour tortilla (folded & browned) w/ham & cheese

singani, *(Bolivia)* alcoholic beverage made from grapes

sin gas, w/out carbonation

sin trabajo, seafood served with the shells removed (means "no work")

sobrasada, salami

sobrebarriga, *(Columbia)* breaded & stuffed steak

soda blanca, *(Costa Rica)* soda water (if bottled water is unavailable)

sofregit, sauteed onions & tomatoes

sofreído, sauteed

sofrito, onions fried w/garlic/sautéed. *(Puerto Rico)* sauté of tomatoes,

onions, red and green peppers, spices, garlic & cilantro.

Commonly found in stews and bean dishes

soja, soy

soldaditos, fried fish sticks

soldat, sole

solla, plaice

solo, neat (straight up) alcoholic beverage

solomillo, fillet steak/tenderloin/sirloin

solomillo andaluz, pork tenderloin

sol y sombra, brandy & anise flavored liquor (means "sun & shade")

sooyosopy, *(Paraguay)* soup of cornmeal,

ground meat, usually served w/rice

Sooyosopy is a Guaraní word which is the other official language of Paraguay.

sopa, soup

sopa a la criolla, *(Peru)* spicy noodle & beef soup

sopa al estilo Mallorca, cabbage soup

sopa alpurrañas, egg & ham soup

sopas cachorreñas, fish soup w/orange zest, vinegar & oil

sopa castellana, vegetable soup/garlic soup w/cumin.

A specialty in the Spanish region of *Castile-Leon*

sopa clara, consommé

sopa criolla dominicana, *(Dominican Republic)* a soup of stewed meat,

greens, onions, spices & pasta

sopa de ajo, garlic soup

ajo .

sopa de ajo blanco, cold soup of garlic, grapes & ground almonds

sopa de albóndigas, chicken broth w/meatballs

sopa de almendras, almond pudding

sopa de aragonesa, soup of calf's liver & cheese topped

w/bread or cheese crust

sopa de calabaza, *(Mexico)* squash soup

sopa de calducho, clear soup

calabaza

sopa de cangrejos, crab bisque

cangrejos.

sopa de cebolla, onion soup

sopa de cocido, meat soup

sopa de cola de buey, oxtail soup

sopa de dátiles, brown mussel soup

sopa de fideos, noodle soup

sopa de frutas de mar, shellfish soup

sopa de galets, pasta & meatball soup

sopa de gallina, chicken soup

gallina.

sopa de gato, garlic soup w/grated cheese

sopa de guisantes, pea soup

sopa de habichuelas negras, black bean soup

sopa de la cena, *(Mexico)* pork sparerib soup

sopa de lentejas, lentil soup

sopa de lima, *(Mexico)* chicken & lime soup

lima.

sopa de maní, *(Bolivia)* roasted peanut soup

sopa de mariscos, shellfish soup. *(Mexico)* tomato, seafood chowder

sopa de mejillones, mussel soup

sopa de mondongo, *(Honduras)* tripe stew or soup

NO THANKS.

sopa de pasta, noodle/pasta soup

sopa de pescado, seasoned fish soup

sopa de picadillo, egg & ham soup

sopa de servillana, spicy fish soup flavored w/mayonnaise

sopa de tomate, tomato soup

tomates.

sopa de tortilla, *(Mexico)* soup of fried
   tortilla strips, chicken & chilies

verduras.

sopa de tortuga, turtle soup

sopa de verduras, vegetable soup

sopa de vino, soup containing sherry

sopa del quarto de hora, soup w/a base of fried onions & rice

sopa espesa, thick soup

sopa liquida, *(Mexico)* "wet soup" or what we in the United States and
Canada think of as soup. See ***sopas secas***

sopa mahimones, soup w/olive oil, bread & garlic base

sopa maimones, soup w/olive oil, bread & garlic base

sopa mallorquina, thick soup of tomatoes, meat,
eggs, onions & peppers

sopa mondongo, *(Nicaragua)* tripe stew

sopa paraguaya, *(Paraguay)* "Paraguayan soup"
mashed cornbread, cheese, onion, milk & eggs

sopa seca, *(Mexico)* rice or pasta covered w/a sauce & served after soup
(means "dry soup"). The second course of a full meal

sopa servillana, spicy fish & mayonnaise soup

sopaipillas, *(Chile)* fried pumpkin

sopapilla, *(Mexico)* deep fried pastry

sope, *(Mexico)* *tortillas* sealed together & filled w/meat or cheese & fried

sorbete, sorbet/cold fruit drink.

  (Columbia) fruit juice w/cream.

  (Central America) ice cream

sospiros de Moros, dry meringues

suave, soft

suero, whey

suflé, soufflé

suizos, breakfast rolls baked w/sugar

supremas de rodaballo, thin slices of fish

suquet, fish & potato stew

surrullitos, *(Puerto Rico)* deep fried corn sticks stuffed w/cheese

surtido, assorted

surubí, *(Paraguay)* a fresh water fish similar to catfish

suspiros, dry meringues. *(Peru)* sweet meringue dessert stuffed w/cream
& often w/fudge

suspiros de monja, soft meringue w/custard

[handwritten note:] Sospiro means Sigh - Sospiros de Moros means Moor's sighs - Sospiros de Monja - A Nun's sighs.

susquet, assorted fish & shellfish stew

susquillo de pescador, assorted fish & shellfish stew

taco, *(Mexico)* meat filled *tortillas* w/tomatoes, onions, & other ingredients.

> *Dorado* means a fried ("U"-shaped hard) *taco* & *suave* means plain (not fried)

un taco.

tajada, slice. *(Latin America)* fried banana slices

tajaditas, *(Nicaragua)* fried banana chips

tallarines, noodles

tallarines a la italiana, tagliatelle

tamale, *(Mexico, Latin America)* corn meal dough filled w/meat & sauce & steamed while wrapped in banana leaves or a corn husk.

> *(Costa Rica)* olives, rice & raisins are often included

tamarindo, tamarind

tapa, snack/appetizer.

> *Tapa* is the Spanish word for lid or cover. The bartender will place an appetizer on top of your glass of wine or beer

Tapas are frequently nuts, olives or meatballs.

tapado, *(Latin America)* stew

tarragón, tarragon

tarrina, en, served in an earthware pot

tarta, cake/tart

Albondigas. (meatballs.)

tarta alaska, baked Alaska

tarta al whisky, whisky & ice cream cake

tarta de arroz, cake containing rice

tarta de Santiago, almond cake

tarta helada, layered ice cream cake

tarta moca, mocha cake

tarta Pasiega, anise flavored cheesecake

tartar crudo, steak tartare

taza, cup

una taza de té.

té, tea

té con leche, tea with milk

té con limón, tea with lemon

té helado, iced tea

tejas, egg white, almond & sugar biscuits

tejos de queso, cheese pastries

tembleque, *(Dominican Republic)* coconut pudding

tenca, tench (an Eurasian fish)

tenedor, fork

Although a Eurasian fish, tench has been introduced to North America and Australia.

tepezcuintle, *(Guatemala)* a Mayan specialty, the largest member of the rodent family

tepín, *(Mexico)* small, very hot chili pepper

tequeños, *(Venezuela)* fried appetizer of dough wrapped around white cheese

tequila, *(Mexico)* ever had a *tequila* hangover? An alcoholic beverage distilled from the pulp of the agave (maguey) plant. Mexican *tequila* is often higher proof than *tequila* sold in the United States and Canada.

Four types are: ***anejo*** (aged in oak barrels for at least one year), ***gold*** or ***joven abocado*** (unaged w/color and flavor added), ***plata*** or ***blanco*** (unaged and sold w/in two months of distilling) and ***reposado*** (aged from two months to one year, means "rested")

Tequila.

tercio, *(Venezuela)* bottled beer

tereré, *(Paraguay)* maté made w/cold water

término medio, medium

ternasco, baby lamb

ternasco asado, lamb roasted in wine & lemons

ternera, veal

terrina, pâté

tetilla, a mild, creamy cheese

tiempo, al, at room temperature (***del tiempo*** means "of the season")

tigres, mussels in cayenne pepper sauce

tila, lime flavored tea

tinto, *(Columbia)* black coffee

tinto de verano, "summer red", red wine w/ lemon-lime soda water

tinto, vino, red wine

tío pepe, a type of sherry

tioro, *Basque* fish soup

típico de la región, regional specialty

tiradito, *(Peru)* fish, lime juice & oil served w/pepper sauce

tisanas, herbal teas

tocinillo de cielo/tocino de cielo, very rich crème caramel

tocino, bacon

todo incluido, all inclusive (price & service)

tojunto, rabbit, meat & vegetable stew

tomate, tomato

tomates rellenos, stuffed tomatoes

tomatillo, *(Mexico)* mild green fruit (similar to a green tomato)

tombet, vegetable stew

tomillo, thyme

tónic/tónica, tonic

tordo, thrush

toro, bull

toronja, grapefruit

torrados, toasted chickpeas

torreja/torrija, french toast/bread dipped in
    milk, fried & sugar coated

torta, cake/breakfast roll topped w/sugar.

    (Costa Rica) meat and/or cheese sandwich.

    (Mexico) a sandwich

[Handwritten notes:]
VINO TINTO! Some of our favorite is Chilean.

tocinillo de cielo was created in the 1600's by Spanish Nuns.

toro!

torta de aceite, plain, bland biscuits *Aceite means oil.*

torta de cielo, almond sponge cake ("cake of heaven")

torta de hojaldre, puff pastry w/jam

torta de plátano, *(Venezuela)* plantain & cheese cake

torta de Santiago, almond cake

torta milanesa, *(Mexico)* deep fried meat sandwich

torta real, "royal cake" w/eggs, almonds & cinnamon

tortells, breakfast roll w/crushed almonds & lemon filling

tortilla, *(Spain)* omelette. *(Mexico)* flat, round cooked unleavened bread. Corn *tortillas* are the daily starch of *Mexico*, made of *masa* (corn flour). In *Northern Mexico*, *tortillas* are often made w/flour

tortilla a la catalana, omelette w/sausage & beans

tortilla a la flamenca, Spanish omelette (see *huevos a la flamenca*)

tortilla a la jardinera, omelette w/mixed vegetables

tortilla a la paisana, omelette w/mixed vegetables

tortilla aliada, omelette w/mixed vegetables

tortilla a su gusto, omelette made w/whatever ingredients you want

tortilla con quesillo, *(Nicaragua)* fried corn *tortillas* w/melted cheese

tortilla de escabeche, omelette containing fish

tortilla de harina, flour *tortilla*

tortilla de huevos, *(Latin America)* omelette

tortilla de jámon, *(Dominican Republic)* a spicy omelette w/ham

tortilla española, omelette w/potato & onion filling

tortilla francesa, plain omelette

tortilla gallega, omelette w/sausage & peppers

tortilla granadina, omelette w/brains, asparagus, peppers & artichokes

tortilla guisada, omelette w/tomato sauce

tortilla hormigos, omelette w/fried breadcrumbs

tortilla murciana, omelette w/tomato & red peppers

tortilla paisana, omelette w/sausage, potatoes, peppers & tomatoes

tortilla piperrada, red pepper, onion & tomato omelette

tortilla Sacramonte, omelette w/sweetbreads

tortita, waffle

tortuga, turtle

tostada, *(Mexico)* fried *tortilla* topped w/ingredients

such as chicken, beans and/or cheese.

(Spain) toast. *(Venezuela)* sandwich w/crisp

bread, meat, cheese or chicken

tostadas de maíz, *(Ecuador)* corn pancakes

tostaditas, *(Mexico)* *tortilla* chips. This can also refer to small *tostadas*

tostado, toasted. **Pan tostado** is toast

tostón, suckling pig

tostones, *(Dominican Republic, Puerto Rico)* fried plantains.

(Venezuela) crisp fried slices of plantains

totopos, *(Mexico)* *tortilla* chips

tournedó, filet steak

toyina, salted tuna

trasero, rump

trigo, wheat

triguillo, turnip soup

tripas, tripe

trozo, rack (as in rack of lamb)

trucha, trout. This is a specialty in *Ecuador*

trucha a la montañesa, trout cooked w/white wine, & bay leaves

trucha a la Navarra, trout cooked w/ham

trucha frita a la asturiana, trout floured & fried in butter

trucha molinera, trout floured & fried w/butter & lemon

trufa, truffle. *Trufado* means w/truffles

truita, omelette

trumfes, potatoes

ttoro, *Basque* fish soup

tuétano, bone marrow

tuna is often called tunny.

trucha.

107

tumbet, vegetable casserole featuring eggplant

tuna, *(Latin America)* prickly pear

tuntas, *(Guatemala)* freeze dried potatoes

turrón, nougat. ***Turrón de guirlache*** is almond brittle

txacoli/txakoli, *Basque* white wine

txangurro, *Basque* dish of seasoned crabmeat

ulloa, a soft cheese similar to camembert

urta, catfish/snapper

utensilio, utensil

uvas, grapes

uvas pasas, raisins

vaca (carne de), beef

vaca salada, corned beef

vainilla, vanilla

vainitas, *(Latin America)* green beans

valenciana, a la, usually means w/tomatoes, rice & garlic

vapor, steamed

variada, bream

variado, assorted

vasca, a la, w/chicken giblets in garlic, parsley & white wine sauce

vaso, glass/tumbler

vegetales, vegetables

vegeteriano, vegetarian. *(Costa Rica)* *"no tiene carne"*
     (literally "does not contain meat") means
     does not have beef, but may contain other meat

venado, venison

veneras, scallops

veracruzana, a la, *(Mexico)* (Veracruz style) w/tomato sauce, capers,
     green olives, onions & yellow peppers

verat, mackerel

verde, *(Mexico)* a common, green, medium-hot pepper

verduras, green vegetables

vermut (vermú), vermouth

vi novell, new wine

similar to Beaujolais Nouveau

vieiras, scallops

villeroy, chicken breasts or prawns

coated in béchamel

vinagre, vinegar

vinagreta, vinaigrette

vino, wine

vino añejo, mature wine

vino blanco, white wine

vino clarete, rosé wine

vino común, table wine

vino de aguja, slightly sparkling white & rosé wines

vino de jerez, sherry

vino de la casa, house wine

vino de la tierra, local wine

vino del país, local wine (wine from the country)

vino de mesa, table wine

vino de Oporto, port

vino de pasto, table wine

vino dulce, dessert wine

vino espumoso, sparkling wine

vino generoso, fortified wine

vino rancio, dessert wine

vino rosado, rosé wine

vino seco, dry wine

vino suave, sweet wine

vino tinto, al, baked in a red wine sauce

vino tinto, red wine

vino tinto. vino blanco.

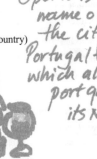

vino de Oporto.

Oporto is the name of the city in Portugal from which all port gets its name.

vino verde, white wine from *Galicia*

viski, whiskey

viudo de pescado, *(Columbia)* fish stew

vizcaína, a la, sauce of peppers, onions, tomatoes, paprika, & garlic

vodka, vodka

vuelvealavida, *(Latin America)* seafood cocktail

whisky, whiskey

whisky americano, bourbon

xampañ, sparkling wine

xerex, another word for *jerez* (sherry)

xató, salad mixed w/tomato, olives,
    anchovies & cod or tuna

xatonada, salad mixed w/tomato,
    olives, anchovies & cod or tuna

xoric amb patates, swallow w/potatoes

xuxos, custard filled doughnuts

yaguarlocro, *(Ecuador)* potato soup w/black pudding (blood sausage)

yema (del huevo), yoke of an egg

yemas, sweet yellow cake/whipped egg yolk.

    (Uruguay) crystallized egg yolk

yerba maté, *(Latin America)* herbal tea

yogur, yogurt

yogur desnatado, low-fat yogurt

yuca, sweet potato.

    (Panama) cassava (an edible root which yields a starch).

    (Dominican Republic) usually boiled or fried & never eaten raw

zamorana, a la, w/cheek of pork & pig's feet

zanahorias, carrots

zanca, shank

zapallo, *(Latin America)* squash

zapote, *(Latin America)* sweet pumpkin

zarangollo, white fish w/tomato & saffron/zucchini & onion casserole

zarzamora, blackberry

zarzuela, assorted seafood stew (highly seasoned)

zarzuela de mariscos, highly seasoned shellfish stew

zarzuela de pescados, highly seasoned seafood stew

zarzuela de verduras, vegetable stew

zoque, cold tomato & pepper soup

zorza, pork fried with paprika

zumo, juice

zumo de fruta fresca, fresh fruit juice

zumo de naranja natural, freshly squeezed orange juice

zurracapote, hot red wine punch w/brandy & cinnamon
or stewed figs & apricots

zurro, white wine cooler

zurrón, stuffed

WINSTON.

Buen Provicho!

Invitation for Comments:

We like to think that we have been as thorough as possible, but we welcome any and all comments, additions and corrections from our readers. You can reach us at:

What Kind of Food Am I?
8223 N. Gray Log Lane
Milwaukee, WI 53217-2863
USA
Fax: 1-414-228-4917
e-mail: EATnDRINK@aol.com

About the Authors:
Michael Dillon, when not operating his graphic design firm, is planning his next meal. Design and illustrations in this guide are the work of Mr. Dillon.

Andy Herbach, when not engaged in the practice of law, is planning his next trip.

Both authors love to eat and travel extensively. They reside in Milwaukee, Wisconsin.